THE
RAVEN
AND THE HAWK

For God and Country,
James A. Danielik

JAMES DANIELIK

THE RAVEN AND THE HAWK
A V8 Designs Book

PUBLISHING HISTORY
V8 Designs softcover first edition published March 2005

Published by
V8 Designs, Studio Arts and Signs
Olongapo City, Philippines

Cover design by
www.ghettodaisy.com
Manuscript layout and production by
www.ghettodaisy.com

Printing by
Primex Printers, Inc.
Mandaluyong City, Philippines

ISBN 971-93247-0-8

Cover and manuscript designed, printed, and manufactured in the Republic of the Philippines.

*Sometimes people unexpectedly stumble into our lives
at the precise moment that we need them to.*

This book is dedicated to one such person.

CONTENTS

1 FIRST MEETING

The sniper's long-range shot split the terrorist's head open like a
ripe watermelon, his brains and blood exploding all over the place.
His lifeless body tumbled out of the top story window he had been
peering out of and fell to the ground.

At least, that's what was in the mind's eye of the watching Congressmen and Senators who held the purse strings
in America's dark new war on the day this story begins.

This is a story I can't tell in complete detail; divulging
those secrets would get me killed. This is not a story of
secret weapons, strategies, tactics, or most of all, names.
In this shadow-world, talk kills, and I've gotten habitu-
ated to breathing.

It is the story of two American boys born a couple of
years and a continent apart, brought together by fate, cir-
cuitous routes or divine intervention. It is a *Forrest Gump*
adventure of two boys who become men, who happened
to be in historic places, during historic times, and who

themselves made history simply by being there.

One was a New York City-born second-generation American whose four grandparents arrived at Ellis Island in the early 1900's by immigrant's ship from Eastern Europe. His father spoke only Polish until he was five years old despite having grown up in New York City. That boy was me.

Years later, after I had earned my pilot's wings in the Air Force, there was a popular television show that detailed the life of a daredevil helicopter pilot. The name of the show was *Airwolf* and the name of the pilot character was Stringfellow Hawke. Believing me to bear a slight resemblance to the Hollywood actor who played the part, someone had the bright idea that I should be called "the Hawk". That became my radio call sign. Since I didn't see myself as a Hollywood actor, I got into the habit of referring to myself in the third person as the Hawk. I'm told it's bad English, but that's the way it is.

The other was a kid adopted by Americans from Washington State. He had some kind of Sioux or Nez Perce Indian blood, which gave him his distinctive chiseled features. I'm not going to give you his real name. As I said before, talk kills.

This is our story and it begins on one of those crisp, clear-blue Carolina days in early winter. Hawk had been tasked with planning and coordinating a Special Operations capabilities demonstration for a congressional delegation.

The assembled Senators and Congressmen would observe highly sensitive air and ground operations at a remote location on the huge military complex at Fort Bragg, North Carolina.

The plan I developed was now coming to fruition. It was execution time and I went to the range to watch the presentation. That is where I began my most coveted relationship with the man known as the Raven.

I didn't know who he was but the first minute I laid eyes on him I knew he was someone unique. Dressed in a black jumpsuit, black assault boots and an American flag attached with Velcro to his sleeve, he stood on top of a berm overlooking an open field that stretched before him. His hair was dark and long, in concert with the relaxed grooming standards popular at the time, but it was his face that was so remarkable. He had the most striking blue eyes I had ever seen, like the deep blue of the Mediterranean Sea. They were completely focused at all times, never wavering, never any doubt, and his stare brought the "steely-eyed killer" cliché to mind. Another officer had commented that he had no lips. That was true. He just seemed to have a grim little line cut between his nose and chin.

There was also a look of sensitivity on that face. He carried his personal demons within and never shared his thoughts or feelings with others, which gave him the reputation of being cold and intimidating. There were reasons and those reasons became obvious to me with deep understanding, after I, too, had been to the dark place he had been.

That day, he was in complete control of himself and the environment around him. There could never be any question in anyone's mind that this man was the epitome of the professional soldier.

I was as captivated by his presence and demeanor as the Senators and Congressman were who stood before him as he commenced his briefing, which he delivered in a strong, steady voice that accentuated the confidence he displayed.

Raven was a troop commander, and his men demonstrated their skills: First, a sniper, hidden in a camouflaged hide-site below the berm, fired a .45-caliber long-gun to blast a dummy terrorist target fitted with a water-filled balloon-head. The dummy was situated in the third-story window of a building fifty meters down range. As the balloon exploded, the loss of the water made the dummy terrorist fall out of the window. Different entry methods to the building using explosives were then explained, with the demonstration culminating in a full-scale assault on the structure by one of Raven's special assault teams.

All the tactics demonstrated could be used in resolving a hostage barricade-type situation. Raven's men were highly trained in advanced marksmanship employing discriminate shooting skills. Enormous amounts of ammunition and time were expended in perfecting their craft. The numerous repetitions resulted in a finely-tuned, razor-sharp soldier who, from close range in the dark, could place two .45- caliber bullets side by side in the forehead of a terrorist holding an American citizen hostage.

As the special activities unfolded before us and the man dressed in black continued his briefing, my only thought was how glad I was to know that this man and his soldiers were Americans. They were our finest military professionals, and I, along with the Senators and Congressmen, was privileged to observe them in action.

The assault was as choreographed as a ballet; however, the music played by the orchestra was replaced by the sounds of explosive charges and muffled gunshot rounds. It was an exhilarating and thrilling experience.

The smell of cordite and the smoke from the explosions hung in the air; and the assault ended as quickly as it had started. That acrid smell, the burning of the eyes and the awful, distinct odor produced only by cordite, an odor you never forget, added to the realism.

After the demonstration, the soldiers formed ranks in front of the structure they had just assaulted, dressed exactly like the man in black. There was, however, one notable difference. These men had their heads and faces covered with balaclavas; black-knitted head coverings which expose only the eyes and mouth. Due to the sensitivity of their mission, these soldiers could not reveal their identities to outsiders.

The Raven then asked the Senators and Congressmen to come forward and meet his men. The VIPs from Washington acted like this was a photo opportunity and rushed forward to meet these special operators. Arms flew all around as the Congressman enthusiastically pumped the hands of the soldiers.

This was an important demonstration because the powerful men from Washington would ultimately disburse the millions of dollars that paid for the massive amount of ammunition, weapons, explosives, target materials and structures used in training these special soldiers. Also, our elected leaders would be instrumental in the employment of this deadly military force. The civilian control of the military was deftly illustrated this day.

The outcome was a resounding success. The congressional delegation returned to Washington knowing full-well in their hearts and minds that the American taxpayers' money was being wisely spent.

As the excitement of the moment expended its energy, and the crowd of people dispersed, the commander known as the Raven just disappeared from view, evaporating like the smoke had. I would not see him for another three months, but it seemed like our lives had become interwoven on that bright winter day.

It was a very exciting time for me. The Hawk had been a transport pilot in the Air Force for eleven years, and he was now flying a desk in his very first staff job; however, this was a staff job like no other. My unit planned, coordinated and executed the infiltration and exfiltration of the special soldiers like those I had seen at the capability demonstration. At my disposal was the mighty United States military arsenal. My primary duty was to coordinate directly with all Department of Defense air units that would support the ground and maritime special operations forces (SOF) in order for them to prosecute their actions on the designated objective.

In the course of these duties, the other ten men in the unit and I became a close-knit bunch of special operators in our own right. There was a Commander and

Deputy Commander who were full Colonels. The Director of Operations was a Lieutenant Colonel, and under him were the action officers, Majors and Captains, of which I, the Hawk, was one.

This unit may not have had the personnel who fired the ultimate two bullets that could snuff out a terrorist's life in an instant, but it would surely get those individuals who fired the fatal shots to the target and safely extract them. The means we used were speed, precision and lethality.

In retrospect, as we hunted terrorists around the world, it seemed especially appropriate that the man dressed in black and I would be named after birds of prey—the Raven and the Hawk.

2 THE FOUNDATION OF ALL TRUTH

As the Raven lay on his back in the rear of the helicopter, choking to death on his own blood, his mind was racing. The previous 12 hours were the most intense moments of his young life, and he felt sure the Grim Reaper had his scythe raised to snuff out the remainder of his weakened life. Little did he suspect that those 12 harrowing hours would result in a Distinguished Service Cross being pinned to his chest.

The Distinguished Service Cross is our nation's second highest award after the Medal of Honor, which is often awarded posthumously. The citation for the Raven's DSC reads as follows:

> *"For extraordinary heroism in connection with military operations involving conflict with an armed hostile force in the Republic of Vietnam: (name classified) distinguished himself on 27 September 1971 while serving as*

a member of a long-range reconnaissance team operating deep in enemy territory. On that date, his team came under attack by an estimated 75- to 100-man force. (He) suffered multiple fragmentation wounds from an exploding B-40 rocket in the initial assault, but despite the serious wounds, placed a deadly volume of machine gun fire on the enemy line. As the enemy advanced, he succeeded in breaking the assault and forced them to withdraw with numerous casualties. When the enemy regrouped, they resumed their assault on the beleaguered team, placing a heavy volume of small arms and automatic weapons fire on his sector of the defensive perimeter. Again he exposed himself to the enemy fire in order to hold his position and prevent the enemy from overrunning the small team. After breaking the enemy assault, the team withdrew to a nearby guard. At the landing zone, (he) refused medical treatment in order to defend a sector of the perimeter, and ensure the safe extraction of his team. (His) extraordinary heroism and devotion to duty were in keeping with the highest traditions of the military service and reflect great credit upon himself, his unit, and the United States Army."

A man is formed by the experiences in his life. Hawk had known the Raven for three years at this point, and yet he said little. "Man of few words" aptly described him. It was the Hawk who always started and ended their conversations. It was like pulling teeth getting him to talk in between.

The first time we discussed this military action was in Hangar Three, sitting on his cot, with about 1,000 other special operations personnel scattered about in various degrees of combat regalia, shooting the bull.

We were preparing to invade a country later that night. Rehearsals were complete, command-and- control documents reviewed, communications links checked, and we were in the abstract world between peace and battle. The Raven and his men were gearing up for a rescue mission they were preparing to execute a few hours later. This mission was one of the most daring yet treacherous ones we had ever planned together.

I did not know if I would see my friend again after that night. The talk was fairly light, but in the back of my mind, I had heard that my friend had performed most heroically in Vietnam some eighteen years earlier. So, right then and there, I asked him point blank about this particular mission that earned him a DSC. I had to know what drives a man to the razors' edge between life and death. The Raven would describe it to me some time later as the ultimate adrenaline rush. He had become a "combat junkie", although his narcotic and needle were war!

The order handed to the Raven that day in Quang Tri, South Vietnam, detailed a cross-border NVA (North Vietnamese Army) "snatch" mission. Raven's superiors needed intelligence on the number of NVA regulars, how much equipment, and the amount of supplies flowing into South Vietnam, and snatching a soldier might provide that required information. Two teams of six men each (four Americans and eight Montagnards) were combined into one and placed under Raven's command for this mission. The Montagnards, Vietnamese hill people from near Khe Sanh, were the best fighters South Vietnam had to offer. The "Yards", as they were known, became integral members of the LRRP (long-range reconnaissance patrol) teams because of their experience and knowledge of the area. The Raven and his eleven-man LRRP team were to be inserted via helicopter west of Tchepone in Laos, near the Ho Chi Minh Trail. The mission was expected to last up to seven days, all behind enemy lines. The quicker the team grabbed someone, the sooner they got out.

Raven and his men prepared their gear, which included one LRRP meal per day. These were prepackaged dried meals that needed water added to resemble something close to a kind of beef stew. The men carefully retaped the seven packages holding the cold meals and put them in their rucksacks. Minimum water was carried, due to its weight and the ability to drink from small mountain streams in the area where they were going to be operating. The men also took their big, pink horse-pills. Otherwise known as "no-shit" pills, they would literally keep the men plugged up as they went into the bush. The Raven swore that the Vietnamese could smell the difference between American shit and the Vietnamese kind. He didn't want the enemy finding him by the fragrance of his waste products!

Into one of the backpacks went a couple of purple smoke canisters. The canisters were used to mark the team's position so the Forward Air Controllers (FACs) could locate them. The FACs, flying in Cessna 172 airplanes, could then direct close-air-support aircraft away from the team's position marked by the purple smoke. The close-air-support aircraft were either the A1 Skyraider (a slow-moving, single prop-driven relic of an aircraft from Korean War days, that carried 2.75" rocket pods, bombs and "twenty-mike-mike" (.20mm) machine guns), or "fast-movers" like F-4 Phantoms. They could both drop "500 pounders" or napalm. If the mission got "hot", and the team needed that close-air-support, they would pull the tabs on top of the canister to release the smoke, and the FACs would do the rest or at least, that was the plan.

Into another team member's rucksack went red and green smoke canisters to mark the extraction zone. When the mission was over, these smoke canisters would be used to signal their location to the helos so they could be flown to safety. Green would be used if the landing zone (LZ) was secure and red, if the LZ was "hot" or under fire.

One other major necessity was thrown into their rucksacks. It was a bottle of pills called "Green Hornets." These pills were amphetamines and would allow the men to stay awake for long periods of time. Raven recalled how he popped them every night he was in the field. Although difficult because of the speed rush, he would then try to get one or two hours of sleep during the day. Raven also remembered grinding his teeth constantly, like a man chewing gum uncontrollably.

The last thing the Raven did was toss his Marlboros away then have his Yards give up their Salems, the brand they were famous for smoking. There would be no puffing on a smoke in the bush. It was far too dangerous. Just like the waste products, the enemy could smell the smoke.

The twelve men lifted off the Quang Tri launch-site in one giant swarm of flying machinery. They were split into two six-man teams aboard two Huey helicopters. Three flying spare Hueys and a chase Huey with a medic on board (call sign "Dustoff") were added to the flight. Spares were added because helos were very vulnerable to small arms fire and many were lost in Vietnam. Four Cobra gunships provided covering fire support.

The formation followed Highway Route Nine east from Quang Tri through Khe Sanh, where the Marines were under siege for five months in 1968, then across the border into Laos. As they neared the LZ, the Cobras prepped the site. They sprayed the area with .20MM cannons and launched 2.75-inch rockets into the sur-rounding jungle. The LZ was near the Ho Chi Minh Trail, which ran north and south, intersecting Highway Route Nine near Tchepone. Feeder routes from the trail flowed east back across the Laotian border toward Khe Sanh and were veritable hotbeds of enemy activity. The NVA used the trail to re-supply and forward position troops through Laos, which was technically "off limits" to the Americans.

It was very late in the afternoon as the two Hueys car-rying the Raven and his men swooped in for a landing. As the men jumped off the skids, one of the Montagnards fell and snapped his wrist. The men picked him up and threw him back on one of the helos before they took off again. This reduced the number on the team to eleven men total, of which only seven were Montagnards. This proved to be a very bad omen. The Yards were very superstitious and having uneven numbers was "bad juju." Only later did they realize how bad the juju really was!

The eleven-man team quickly moved into the tree-line abutting the open area LZ. They found a small knoll contained by the nastiest surroundings; small bushes, bamboo, double canopy trees, and dense jungle. The knoll provided them the best protection and a lay-up position for the night.

Unfortunately, the small team was immediately detected by two NVA trackers. The trackers were alerted by the sounds of roaring engines and whirling rotor blades. The monotonous but soothing "whop-whop" sounds were just beginning to fade away, replaced by the ominous sounds of the hunters seeking the hunted, as the trackers focused on the team's position.

As darkness began to fall, the LRRP team prepared their defensive perimeter for the night. Approaching midnight, there was a significant increase in movement and sound nearby.

Unknown to Raven and his men, the trackers had left and returned with an NVA company composed of 75 to 100 fighters. The enemy NVA company moved into positions close to where the Raven's team was trying to hide.

Now fully alert, the Raven's senses were on heightened awareness in the pitch black early-morning hours. He began to hear the voices of the enemy clearly and distinctly. It was as if they had become part of his team and seemed only a few meters away. This was when the "ne gotiations" commenced. The Yards became the Raven's interpreters during this intense negotiating period.

The NVA had their own Yards, which Raven's men referred to as VC (Viet Cong) Yards or enemy Yards. The Montagnards have their own language, different from Vietnamese.

The VC Yards started jabbering, which sounded to the Raven like squawking jaybirds, as they promised not to kill Raven's Yards if they surrendered their Americans. The NVA never took a Montagnard prisoner. They would kill them first and ask questions later.

Tempting Raven's Yards to give up the Raven and his fellow Americans, the VC Yards were promising the NVA would not harm them. This was relayed to Raven, and the classic World War II response "Nuts!" came to mind. However, he was a 24-year-old American, old by Vietnam War standards, and serving his second one-year tour of duty. At the time, the average age of an American soldier serving in Vietnam was 19, with only a high school education. He instructed his Yards to respond to the enemy, in so many words, "Fuck you." Perhaps that's what that U. S. Army General really told the Germans during the Battle of the Bulge instead of "Nuts!"

Just before daylight, around 5:30, the screeching sound of two shoulder-launched B-40 rockets pierced the air as they slammed into the team's position. Shrapnel from the exploding warheads wounded every single member. One Yard took a piece in his head and died within 15 minutes.

As he related the story to me, the Raven referred to this horrific encounter as the Purple Haze mission. I asked him why such a name, and he told me that in the initial rocket assault a fragment entered the one man's rucksack with the purple smoke canisters and ignited one of them. As the purple smoke drifted over the team's position during the battle, it only added an eerie spectacle to the vicious fighting. However, the purplish cloud was inevitably etched into each man's mind. A popular song playing on the radio at the time, recorded a year previously by the late Jimi Hendrix, was *Purple Haze*. Whenever the Raven and his recon mates ever discussed this battle, they referred to it as "the *Purple Haze* mission".

Flying pieces of metal punctured Raven's legs, making them look like Swiss cheese. As he faced the direction the rockets came from, the first wave of enemy assaulted his position. The Raven opened fire with his Chinese-made, sawed-off barrel RPD machine gun. NVA began falling from the thunderous hail of Raven's bullets. When the assault turned to retreat, nearly two dozen of the enemy soldiers lay dead or dying on the landscape.

During the assault, the Raven took an enemy AK-47 round in the head which entered his left cheek an inch below his eye (the bullet remains lodged under his right eye today). The round went through a piece of bamboo before it got him which no doubt saved his life. Part of the bullet broke off, and he only took the remaining half of the round in his face.

The initial assault was repulsed and the Raven was completely unaware of his wounds until he began to choke on the blood which was filling his sinus. He looked over at one of his American soldiers, nicknamed Frenchy, and asked him how he looked. Frenchy responded succinctly and without emotion, "Ah, you'll live."

The enemy regrouped for another assault. This time the team was overrun and the fighting was at point-blank range. One NVA soldier who ran right over the Raven, was shot, and ran another four steps before crumpling to the ground. Raven referred to this phenomenon as the "Running Dead." Raven had expended his primary weapon's ammo and resorted to his pistol.

He killed an additional five NVA. One was a Captain whom he shot in the forehead from four feet away. His pistol empty, he pulled out his knife and killed one more by plunging it into the man's upper chest. The second assault was broken, and the enemy retreated into the bush to lick their wounds and count their dead. There were over 60 bodies lying outside and inside the team's perimeter.

Although the end result was the same, this was not the surreal kind of war we all saw on television during Desert Storm in the Persian Gulf. No smart bombs were dropped from high altitude with precision guidance systems to destroy bunkers, tanks or whole buildings. This war was more personal, yet just as lethal and deadly.

The Raven grabbed a Russian-made AK-47 Kalashnikov weapon from a dead enemy soldier and moved his men back to the LZ for helo extraction. Disregarding his own serious wounds, he took up a defensive position to ward off a final assault by the NVA.

As the Hueys came in to extract Raven's team, a

firestorm of small arms and automatic weapons fire destroyed two helos on the LZ. Three of the eight crewmen were killed. Raven's team and the remaining five crew members loaded into two more helos. These two helos were shot up so badly they had to land just over the Lao-Vietnamese border. One helo carried a dead pilot; shot in the head, his brain was scattered all over the cockpit windscreen. The copilot, who was wounded in the shoulder, remained at the controls. In addition to the firefight on the ground, an A1E Skyraider flying close-air-support was shot down by 37mm fire, killing the pilot.

As he was being flown back to Quang Tri in the helicopter, the battle started to recede from his mind, and the Raven became acutely aware of his wounds. Lying on his back on the helo floor, he started to panic and flail about, almost drowning in the blood from his wounded face. Later, two more of his team died from the wounds they had received during the battle.

The Raven's foundation of truth was quite different from mine. While I was growing up in the drug-induced, free-love spirit of the late '60s and early '70s in the good ol' USA, the Raven was experiencing a more sinister lifestyle in some shit-hole half-way around the world.

That day, on the cot in that hot and humid hangar, I had only gotten the partial story. Yes, he had been in Vietnam and had gotten a DSC for gallantry in action, but he had not given the story this kind of detail-only that he had been wounded and fought off a company of NVA soldiers. The details only came out later due to my ruthless grilling of the man, but he did share them with me, cementing my admiration for him forever.

Many years later, he sent me a short note which summed up some of his personal feelings about Vietnam. The words read, "Friend, when a man lives with a gun beside him for a long time knowing it's the only thing between him and hell, he comes to savor every moment, albeit in a quiet and circumspect way. The trouble is that most of us live in anticipation or in memory, not in the present. There are times when you must sit still and listen, feel, see - let the chaos going on around you pass because part of your soul belongs to the blood-soaked ground of Vietnam and we'll never get free from its clutch." Heavy shit!

Although I didn't go to church or discuss religion with the Raven, I found out again many years later where his head was. We saw some movies together and heard a line from one that said "There are no atheists in a foxhole." The Raven, who was a very private man and had been "in the shit" often, confirmed that for me. This man also shared that one of his favorite TV shows was *Touched by an Angel*. I thought this was incredibly ironic. A man who had seen so much death, devastation and destruction believed in prayer, miracles and angels!

The Raven reluctantly shared the total picture with me over a long period of time. He held it within his soul for twenty-seven years, and now I somewhat knew what dragons had lured him to their lairs.

3 MURPHY STRIKES

Hawk is in an abandoned B-52 alert facility at an East Coast location. As the United States prepared for the ultimate nuclear battle with the Soviet Union, many of these bases were built, funded and fueled by nuclear hysteria. Now it was just another relic of the Cold War.

The base was located in Georgia and was being used in the fight against terrorism and Military Operations Other than War (MOOW), the new asymmetric threats that were becoming prevalent in this dangerous new world order.

My unit was hunkered down in the underground bunker. A requirement to move a small team of Special Forces into a simulated hostile third-world country was brought to the air planners. The type of aircraft to be used, the takeoff time, the route to be flown and the destination airfield were coordinated and deconflicted from other on-going missions. The team leader who came to receive the mission briefing was the Raven.

It had been some time since I had seen him, and we had not yet established our friendship; however, my mission was to support him. He defined the mission requirements, and I planned and coordinated a complex air operation to meet his needs.

I took great pride in my job and treated his mission with the same precise, detailed planning of any other. I was to cover every contingency and ensure the aircrew flying the mission knew the plan and flew the plan. I wanted the pilots to have all the necessary information so there would be no misunderstanding that could lead to a disaster of national proportions. Coming on the heels of Desert One in Iran, we had to have 100% success. The American public would stand for nothing less.

If any details were missed, highly skilled and highly trained people would get killed. These, as some may remember, were the relatively early days of night vision goggle (NVG) flying. Pilots were using PVS-5s, the Model T of enhanced vision at night. The stress of flying with these goggles limited the flying time to three hours. The acuity was so very sensitive that the larger Air Force C-130 and C-141 aircraft required three pilots in the cockpit. The aircraft commander, in the left seat, could only focus his goggles to look outside for obstructions along the route and the airfield's runway during landing. The co-pilot, in the right seat, was focused on the instruments inside as he mainly flew the plane. The safety pilot, who sat between them, had one eye focused outside to back up the pilot and one adjusted inside to help monitor the instruments. The "jump seater", as he was known, was usually a young co-pilot. The left- and right-seaters had at least five years' flying experience each, thousands of hours of flying time and certainly had every specialized qualification, including airdrop and air refueling.

Now, imagine a 707-sized aircraft hurtling through the night sky at 300 knots, just 500 feet above the ground, all internal and external lights blacked out. At the controls, young American pilots carried one of the most lethal and dangerous cargoes in the American arsenal, the Army Special Forces belonging to Raven's unit.

Because the technology of NVG flying then was in quite a primitive state, there was a learning curve, as in any undertaking. Unfortunately, the learning curve was steep, and paid for with American lives. From Desert One in Iran to numerous training accidents that the American public would never hear about, both Special Ops aircrew members and operators readily sacrificed themselves in this new form of surrealistic warfare.

The "shooters" first employed the use of NVGs. The guys whose job is to put two bullets side by side in your forehead could do this in total darkness with the goggles aiding their vision. Some bright and shiny pilot who had been exposed to this technology then applied it to flying.

As a matter of fact, one unit's motto was "Death Waits in the Dark" and another's was "Darkness Brings Death." The "flyers" were deliverers of death at night! They were masters of the black shadows, but it took time and came at the expense of some gifted and talented pilots and aircrew members.

As the Hawk, it was incumbent upon me to reduce or

totally eliminate the human cost. Therefore, excruciating attention was given to every mission, whether one aircraft or a multi-ship formation. Every detail was painstakingly reviewed and briefed prior to execution.

Another one of our popular sayings at the time was "there are no stupid questions." Anybody who didn't understand the mission profile could ask any question at any time without fear of ridicule or reprisal. We wanted everybody to understand the mission profile, from the lowest-ranking airman or soldier riding the aircraft to the Generals that were the overall warlords of the operation.

We were in line with the tradition of Napoleon's corporal. Napoleon was asked why he had a corporal in his tent when briefing his war plans and he responded, "If this corporal understands the plan then everybody in rank above him should also."

This was what the times were like when the Raven came to my shop for support of his mission. The aircraft selected to fly the mission was a small two-engine prop. It carried two pilots and a small team. The mission was to infiltrate the team to an airfield in the backwoods of South Carolina. The profile was fairly straightforward. Take off, rig for night running by taping the instruments with infrared masking tape, don goggles, fly at tree-top level, and land at an airfield with no lighting, disgorge the passengers, depart and return to base. I felt confident about the mission and continued with planning the details of other follow-on flights.

I did not know how close I came to having a fatal accident on my watch until a few days later, after the Raven and his team had been picked up and exfiltrated to our location. He came to the underground bunker for a debriefing. This was another remarkable display of the total self-control by the Raven that became commonplace in our years of service together.

Unbeknown to me, Murphy had struck. You know Murphy. (Murphy's Law - If it can go wrong, it will!) He is the guy who shows up and throws a monkey wrench into the plan and messes with your head. You think you have all the bases covered, but then, up pops Murphy. He can be a dangerous SOB. He makes the axiom "The best-laid plans often go awry" all too often a reality.

The Raven commenced his debrief of the mission and said everything was on track, as far as he was concerned, through the landing phase. He was seated behind the pilots and watched the landing with a pair of his own NVGs. The infiltration of his team was going uneventfully until the rollout after landing. As the plane decelerated, a large fire truck loomed in their path as they came down the runway. The pilots quickly swerved around the truck blocking the airstrip. The Raven remarked that he remembered seeing people diving off and running away from the fire truck. Those firemen were probably as shocked as the pilots to find each other occupying the same space at the same time. They were just trying to avoid getting burned up in a fireball if the airplane had collided with their fire truck.

The Raven was also on headset monitoring the pilot's conversation, preparing to exit the aircraft with his team, when the pilot taxied them to the exact offload position.

The offload position had to be exact in order for the team to get their ground orientation start point for their mission in darkness. He heard the pilot make the classic comment "Aw shit!" He reported that the conversation which followed sounded a lot like this: "Is everybody all right?" "Whew, that was fucking close!" "What the fuck was that motherfucking fire truck doing there?"

As the pilots' heart rates were trying to downshift from overdrive, a sudden realization came over them that they might have screwed the pooch. People flying blacked-out airplanes at night have to either have some smarts or be totally crazy, probably a little of both. This was dangerous stuff and their minds were racing powerfully from the adrenaline rush they had just received, fast-asking themselves "who, what, where, when, why, and how."

Why is a fire truck out there? Well, for very good safety reasons. A fire truck is pre-positioned at the field in case of an aircraft accident. Having the truck nearby can mean the difference between life and death in burning wreckage. Statistics report that most people who die in an aircraft accident do so from smoke inhalation or the fire itself, as opposed to the crash impact itself. If having the fire truck nearby can reduce the reaction time to an accident site and a life is saved, then we add a fire truck to the plan.

In this case, the fire truck was pre-positioned near the runway; however, it was parked on the parallel taxiway. The pilots had accomplished the unthinkable--they had landed on the taxiway instead of the runway and almost killed a slew of people!

The Raven understood the risks and knew that mistakes were going to be made, but he just reported them matter-of-factly and moved on with the "mish."

As I watched him relate the story, I was totally surprised yet enthralled by his composure. Instead of storming into the bunker and telling everybody they were AFU (all fucked up), he just delivered a professional after-action report. This would help everybody in the future. Procedures would be changed; safety distances measured and increased; and we would become a better and safer force.

This was another reason why I admired the man in black. He was a warrior, but he was also a statesman, one whom people looked to for superior guidance. He could articulate tactics, techniques and procedures, as well as practice their deadly arts. Again we were placed together by our common love of the counterterrorist mission for which we were preparing our lives. The time was fleeting, but another memory became tucked away.

4 ACHMED AND THE JACKALOPE

It's funny how things work out sometimes. My next mission with the Raven was nearly a duplicate of the previous one, with less drama and more humor.

We were in a hangar at an Air Force base in the high desert of Southern California. The scenario was that a commercial aircraft packed with civilians from Germany, Britain and the United States had been hijacked by terrorists into a hostile third-world country. The terrorists had sorted the passengers according to their nationality and proceeded to hide the American and British hostages at two remote locations while the German citizens remained on board the aircraft.

Through delicate negotiations with our allies, the British sent their counterterrorist unit, 22 SAS, and the Germans sent GSG-9, their elite border guards. The Americans sent the Raven and the Hawk.

The overall plan was for each unit to conduct a si

multaneous assault on each hostage location and the hijacked aircraft. The Germans were selected to assault the aircraft based on their recent success in rescuing their citizens from an airplane that had been hijacked to Mogadishu, Somalia. The Americans and the Brits were to be infiltrated to a remote desert location with all-terrain vehicles, conduct a cross-country movement, and link up with small reconnaissance teams observing the targets. The Germans would conduct a high-altitude parachute jump some distance from the airfield where the hijacked airplane was being held and proceed on foot to a hide-site near the airfield.

At the appointed time, all three assault forces would conduct integrated operations against their respective targets, neutralize the terrorists, and rescue the hostages. The British and American assault teams would load their hostages onto their vehicles and drive to the airfield where GSG-9 had successfully "taken down" the aircraft. A number of military aircraft would then be flown in to the airfield to pick up the hostages and their rescuers.

The Ravens' NCOIC (non-commissioned officer in charge) came to the air planner's area with a validated requirement to infiltrate their team and a civilian looking van into an airfield in Arizona. The mission was to rescue a CIA operative in the simulated hostile country who had passed information on the whereabouts of the hostages. The CIA agent's cover had been blown in the process, and he was now holed up in a safe house.

The NCOIC had also been on the Murphy mission with the Raven and was still a little wide-eyed from that

fateful excursion. That look had now become a perma-
nent part of his facial expression. One can imagine what
he was thinking when the Raven explained to him the
mission requirements. Now he shows up at my desk asking to be subtly infiltrated again! The same guys are asking for the same mission profile from the same mission
planner, hoping lightning wouldn't strike twice!

Lessons were learned from the previous faux pas and
a safety factor was added. A combat controller (an Air
Force NCO) would somehow get to the airfield prior
to any mission aircraft being flown in to it and provide
terminal guidance to the pilots. His mission was to put
eyes on the airfield from a remote location and make a
radio call to the inbound aircraft confirming the field
was safe for landing. He would ensure that there were no
obstacles, vehicles or other potentially aircraft-damaging
objects blocking the runway. He could also tell the aircraft
to discontinue its approach and landing if the aircraft was
misaligned with the runway or he might prevent some
other catastrophe should circumstances suddenly change.

The combat controller selected for this mission was a
young sergeant with long hair, squinty eyes, a large nose
and a Fu Manchu moustache. At the briefing, the aircrew
gave him the nickname "Achmed, the Yankee-lover."

"Achmed" had shown up wearing a long robe tied with
a piece of braided rope to secure it and an Arabic kaf-
fiyeh covering his head. This is the checkerboard head-
dress which was a distinctive trademark of former terrorist turned statesman, the late Yasser Arafat. The young
NCO was getting into the spirit of the moment and was

bringing his bit of realism to the mission.

"Achmed" was quietly flown in a privately chartered aircraft to the airbase in Arizona where Raven's team was to arrive. When "Achmed" got off the aircraft, the airfield commander, an Air Force Lieutenant Colonel, met him.

During these relatively new days of counterterrorist training, there was a certain mystique and aura surrounding our organization. We had a new mission; we looked different from the mainstream military; and people didn't know how to deal with or react to us. We came storming onto bases and made numerous demands on behalf of the US Government. We were "long hairs" in suits and ties, reading selected individuals into our mission and making them sign documents swearing them to secrecy. They became co-conspirators and were sucked into the magic of the moment themselves.

On this day, the Lieutenant Colonel became part of that lore. Usually, we never gave our ranks to outsiders when we were introduced, so that subordinate personnel who wanted to ask questions of their superiors were never intimidated by the rank structure. Remember, there are no stupid questions in this business!

When the Lieutenant Colonel met "Achmed" early that evening as he deplaned, he promptly drove him straight to the Officer's Club and bought him dinner. The officer had been read into the mission and signed the secrecy document. The officer never questioned the young man's rank, assuming the guy had to be an officer or somebody of high importance because of his appearance and dress. We weren't trying to pull one over on anybody, but things like this just happened. It was fun and we had a laugh, but never at anybody's expense. We just felt like little school kids who got away with hiding the teacher's chalk.

The Lieutenant Colonel dropped off the now well- fed "Achmed" near the runway later that evening. "Achmed" set up his radios, made contact with the inbound MC-130 Talon, and cleared the aircraft to land in the pitch-black Arizona night. The aircraft landed fully blacked out, came to a stop, and opened the rear cargo door, and a van full of "shooters" drove out the back. The Raven and his team were successfully infiltrated without incident. The vehicle loaded with Raven's team then drove through a prearranged open gate which had been coordinated by the young sergeant with the base commander. "Achmed" then hopped on the aircraft, the doors were closed and the plane departed, never to be seen or heard from by the airfield commander again. The aircraft just appeared and disappeared completely in a matter of minutes.

The Raven and his men drove 100 miles down the road in their vehicle, placed it in a hide-site and moved into their observation posts overlooking the safe house in another remote desert location.

It was late at night now, in the desert, and the team member's minds started to play tricks on them. They heard a few bushes rustling, some guttural and hissing sounds and thought, quite possibly, a hungry cougar was in the area searching for a meal. Here are our hearty warriors: armed to the teeth, dressed in black ninja suits, wearing night-vision devices looking like something out of *Star Wars* and they were sweating out the possibility of being attacked and eaten by a wild beast.

The wide-eyed NCO who initially came to me with the mission requirements was known as "the Slammer." Slammer had previously been on a cold-weather training exercise in Jackson Hole, Wyoming. During an off day, Slammer drove into town and went into one of the ski shops there, which was selling a stuffed creature called the "Jackalope." Somebody mischievously took the horns of an antelope and glued them to the head of a jackrabbit, which has those extra long ears just like a burro, and called it a Jackalope.

Suddenly, out of the bushes, one of the swift and ferocious beasts charged through the positions of our heroes. Weapons drawn, ready to blast the beast, the men found themselves staring into the beady, red eyes of a wild burro. The team had mistakenly set up their observation positions near the grazing area of a pack of wild burros and had disturbed their habitat.

This particular burro had no fear of the intruders and was making a hissing statement, trying to get the strangers to leave. The gutsy burro became known as the ferocious "Jackalope" and it was doing its best to create a disturbance in order to scare the Raven and his team away. Slammer was the one who gave the name "Jackalope" to the wild burro that attacked our fearless warriors' position. In the dark, Slammer thought the beast looked just like that strangely-modified creature he had seen in the ski shop.

Fortunately, no shots were fired and the men moved on to link up with the CIA agent and take him to safety.

The "Jackalope" safely returned to his pack and all was right with the world again. This was how "Achmed" and the "Jackalope" became part of the Raven and Hawk story.

5 THE FIELD MARSHAL'S LIEUTENANTS

As the first rocket screamed through the Iranian night sky, the guards did not have time to react or escape from their towers overlooking the compound holding British hostages. The two structures became towering infernos and their ensuing collapse took the guards to their deaths.

The mission that brought the Raven and the Hawk together more closely, since we were more or less thrown together by the Fates, led us to another garden paradise.

It had been eighteen months since our first operation together, but this one lasted ten days and we became the equivalent of what were once called blood brothers.

Blood brothers were the kind of friends you had grown up with, playing Cowboys and Indians or King of the Hill. You made lasting pledges to each other about being friends for life, would prick your fingers with needles to draw blood and then touch them together. Although the Raven and I had become closer during this short time together and could almost be referred to as buddies, between us there still remained a certain distance.

A NATO P-3 Orion, carrying a mixed American and British aircrew and nuclear-tipped torpedoes, strayed across the Turkish-Iranian border. The Iranians shot the P-3 down and the mixed crew suffered some casualties. The surviving crewmembers were sorted by nationality and split into two locations. The bodies of the dead crewmembers and the nuclear devices were co-located with the British hostages.

The Iranians attempted to negotiate the release of the British and American crewmembers separately by playing one country against the other, making demands of one country in order to force the other country to capitulate. The demands were quite high – US $5 million per crew member and $20 million for each nuclear-tipped torpedo. However, the thought of a rogue nation like Iran being in possession of any kind of nuclear device and the technology that could be gained was too enormous a risk for the United States and Britain. A hostage-rescue mission was determined to be the best course of action.

Through high-level intelligence sources, the locations of the hostages, bodies and devices were somewhat pinpointed. The British government was determined to save its personnel, and committed all its resources to a rescue operation. However, knowing its resources were limited, a request was made to the Americans for assistance. Who did they call? None other than the Raven and the Hawk and our circle of deadly friends!

We were flown into a cold and rainy European location. The planning areas and sleeping accommodations were old World War II bunkers.

The leader of this lethal package, sent by the U.S. government, was an Army Colonel, known as the Panther. The Panther was an incredibly intelligent and thoughtful commander. He was also known to have a very dry and sometimes sarcastic wit. When a Washington Post writer attempted to interview the Panther on the phone, he was told, "The Colonel does not have a spokesman, but if I did, I would tell him to say, 'The Colonel has no comment on that: as a matter of fact, he does not even acknowledge he exists.'" He had an ever-present cigar jutting out of his mouth. He briefed with it. He even ran with it in his mouth during physical training (PT). I don't ever remember seeing him without it. I swear he probably slept with it. He was quite the sight; however, he was a brilliant thinker and tactician. He was a noted historian of war and strategy, and patterned himself after other great Army leaders, notably Patton and MacArthur. He didn't have the pearl-handled pistols or the aviator glasses and corncob pipe, but he had his cigars.

The first time we all met in his war room, the Panther looked at the Raven and me, with the stogie dangling out of his mouth, and told us we were in charge of putting the ground tactical plan and the supporting air plan together. He explained to us that he, the Colonel, was the Field Marshal, overseer of the "Big Picture" and we were his lieutenants, expected to turn his vision into battlefield glory. He must have been caught up in the moment and our surroundings, because we were in the Year of Our

Lord 1987, and not World War II. He was not Rommel and we were not Afrika Korps and Panzer Division lieutenants, but I think that at that first meeting, he convinced us we were.

The next ten days were a blur, but was one of the most fucking awesome times of my life. The man in black, known only fleetingly by me before, and I were given the tremendous responsibility of representing our nation in a time of crisis and expected not to fuck-up.

The Raven and the Hawk were probably two of the most powerful majors in the US Army and Air Force at the time. Why do I say this? Well, can you imagine having at your disposal a squadron of the Raven's special soldiers and an equivalent squadron from the British 22 SAS? In addition, we had a battalion of British Paratroopers commanded by Lt. Col. Farrah-Hockley, son of Sir General Anthony Farrah-Hockley, a noted hero of the British-Indian War and author of The Edge of the Sword, about being a POW in the Korean War.

A British aircraft carrier, the Ark Royal, and a British submarine were maritime platforms available for our use, and the air package was incredibly awesome. The Royal Air Force provided six giant C-130 Hercules air transports and the U. S. added an additional three. The Royal Air Force also had four large Chinook CH-47 helicopters at our beck and call.

The U. S. Army brought eight troop-carrying, air-assault UH-60 Blackhawks and eight "Little Birds". The "Little Birds" were split into four AH-6s and four MH-6s. The AH-6s were modified Bell 500 helicopters with a specially mounted 7.62 mini-gun and a fourteen- round, 2.75 HE (high explosive) rocket pod. These little whirling dervishes had their own special name - "Killer Eggs.

The MH-6s had flat pods mounted on the side, which enabled them to carry four to six troops. The "Slicks", as they were known, could also have specially modified seats attached to their sides to carry snipers for long-range shooting with pin-point accuracy.

All of these assets were ours to rehearse and use to accomplish the mission. All the crews flying the aircraft would ultimately be under my control, as I coordinated the entire air plan in order to support the ground tactical plan. Likewise, all the ground forces (the Army Special Forces, the British SAS and the British paratrooper battalion) would be under the Raven's control. A renowned Hollywood director once said a movie set is the biggest toy box in the world. He was wrong!

After the first day of receiving the mission and meeting the commanders of the various air, ground and maritime units, the Raven and the Hawk commenced to work out the details of the operation. We had nine days to plan, rehearse and execute the mission to rescue the hostage crewmembers, secure the nuclear devices and return the dead crewmembers to their respective homelands.

The Raven's initial objective was to get human eyes on the targets. From his Vietnam background, he understood the importance of advance force operations. He had been a recon guy a long time before he went through selection for his special unit. Several reconnaissance and surveillance (R&S) teams were assembled from the British SAS and the Raven's unit. The teams were thoroughly briefed on the objectives of their mission.

They were loaded aboard the British submarine and used the stealth of the underwater craft to get close to the Iranian shore. As the submarine approached land as nearly as possible, she momentarily surfaced. The R & S teams inflated four black combat-rubber-raiding-craft (CRRC) called "Zodiacs" and mounted small trolling motors on the back.

The Zodiacs could fit about six men each. Two primaries and two spares with drivers ferried the recon teams to shore. Once safely on shore, the Zodiacs and their drivers returned to the mother sub ship, dismounted the motors, deflated and stowed the boats and the submarine returned to its natural hiding place under water. Under cover of darkness, the recon teams traveled overland to three target sites.

The intelligence types, who used their satellites to make initial estimates on the whereabouts of the crew-members, gave us the supposed hostage locations.

One of the target sites that an R & S team was to observe was an airfield right on the coastline. This was a very important subject for me on which to gather information. The plan required an airfield seizure package to secure a runway for the hostages, nuclear devices, dead bodies and rescue teams to fly out from once all were safely recovered. The airfield seizure package consisted of nine British and American C-130 aircraft filled with approximately 600 of England's finest light infantry forces, the Paras of Lt. Col. Farrah-Hockley.

The plan had an H-Hour established that allowed all three targets (the two hostage/device sites and the airfield) to be hit simultaneously.

The remaining two recon teams found their way to the two hostage locations and put their eyes on the facilities holding the aircrew and nuclear torpedoes. Carrying long-range satellite communications, the teams sent situation reports (sitreps) back to our location. These "sitreps" provided us the best data for our planning purposes.

The information we needed to know was the number of guards and roving patrols, the changeover times, any vehicles and vehicle movements, and the type construction of the facilities holding our hostages. The Raven and I tailored our force packages in order to bring about the most lethal firepower on each target.

Over the course of the next few days, the Raven and I spent quite a bit of time together. When two guys are given the responsibility we were, it would only follow that we would pick each other's brain to the fullest extent. This included learning about each other in a more personal manner. We discovered we had some similarities and common traits.

Although we were from opposite sides of the country, the Raven from Washington State and I from New York, we were close in age (two years apart), so we both had spent our formative years in the turbulent '60s. We found out that we had both been enlisted in our respective services, and had received our commissions as officers by being "90-day wonders". We were both married and each had three kids that were all nearly equal in age. These personal revelations actually helped define one to the other.

The plan had to have a synergistic effect and the Raven and the Hawk supported each other's thought processes in order to come to a successful resolution. The solution had to be perfect. The Field Marshal's lieutenants could not and would not fail!

The seizure of the Iranian airfield was the key to the success of the mission. The airfield was the receiving point of the British and American Special units and their "Precious Cargo" (PC). The nine C-130s departed from an airfield in a friendly country in the Persian Gulf, flew a preplanned route under cover of darkness and landed in a covert manner at the Iranian airfield.

The British landed their first C-130s using night-vision goggles, and unloaded combat controllers to command and control all follow-on operations. The CCT directed the remaining C-130s to land on the runway, where the giant airlifters momentarily stopped, opened their cargo doors and lowered the ramp to offload the British paratroopers and their ground assault vehicles. Upon completion of the offload, the C-130s raised their ramps and the CCT directed them to their parking positions on the airfield.

The phenomenal tactic that the British aviators used, which surprised even us Americans (who would normally boast of superior equipment and tactics), was the simultaneous landing of two C-130s. One aircraft touched down half way down the field and the other at the leading edge of the primary landing runway. This would put maximum fire power on the ground almost instantaneously in two separate locations, providing additional speed, surprise and lethality.

The assault was such a complete surprise that the Iranians defending the field were overwhelmed in a matter of minutes. The paratroopers under the command of Farrah-Hockley then moved out and secured the airfield perimeter. The airfield was ready to receive the helicopters from their respective targets.

The 22 SAS squadron was loaded aboard the British carrier, the Ark Royal, and given the British Chinooks for airlift support. In addition, two American "Little Bird" AH-6 gunships were added for fire support. This force cruised close to the Iranian shore and launched from the deck of the ship to fly straight to the Brit target.

At their target, the 22-SAS soldiers "neutralized" the Iranian guards, secured the nuke-tipped torpedoes and dead crewmembers, and rescued the British flyers. The soldiers had to hit three separate buildings within the enemy compound. Each Chinook carried the troops required to secure each building. The three helos flew together to a rendezvous point (RP), then split up, swooped down onto their respective targets, quickly offloaded their troops and flew back to the RP and waited to be called back in for exfiltration. The SAS soldiers were coolly efficient and secured all three targets within minutes. There were two guard towers overlooking the enemy compound, but two well-placed 2.75-inch rockets from the "Killer Eggs" resolved that situation immediately.

Upon completion of the SAS actions on their objective, the Chinooks were called back in and the troops, hostages, nuclear torpedoes and dead crewmembers were uploaded. They linked up with the AH-6s and flew to the transload airfield. The two AH-6s had to drop in for gas at the refueling site en route to the airfield. After reaching the airfield and completing the transload of their PC, the five helos flew back and recovered aboard the Ark Royal. Because the 22 SAS soldiers were responsible for recovering the nuclear torpedoes, and the possibility existed that the weapons had been damaged in the shoot-down, all rescue forces (troops and helo crews) had to go through a decontamination process aboard the Ark Royal. This included a complete scrub-down of all personnel and disposal of their uniforms by incineration.

The American Special Forces flew to their target in the American Blackhawks. Five UH-60s launched from an island in the Persian Gulf close to the Iranian coast and flew under cover of darkness to their target. Upon reaching the target, the helos tactically offloaded the American soldiers at designated helicopter landing zones (HLZs) in close proximity to the buildings where the American crewmembers were being held hostage. After offload, the helos flew to "on call" positions. When the Raven's special soldiers had secured their hostages, the helos were called back in to upload everyone and fly to the transload airfield.

Two additional UH-60s landed in the Iranian desert and established a Forward Area Refueling Position (FARP). These aircraft carried the extra fuel and the hoses needed to dispense it, in order for the five other Blackhawks to fly to their target, loiter at the target and then stop for a much-needed gulp of gas en route to the airfield.

Upon reaching the airfield, the PC was transloaded to the C-130 designated to carry the nuclear weapons, hostages and any wounded or dead personnel. The Black-hawks then refueled from a C-130 FARP at the airfield and returned to their island launch site. The PC C-130 flew to an RAF base in Cyprus for medical attention, decontamination and turnover of sensitive devices and bodies to respective American and British government officials.

After the PC C-130 departed the Iranian airfield, Lt. Col. Farrah-Hockley directed the collapse of the perimeter and commenced exfiltration operations. At the completion of the roll up of all the 3rd Paras and their vehicles, the remaining eight C-130s departed and flew back to their original launch airfield.

This operation was a huge success with no loss of life or equipment. We recovered not only the hostages and the bodies of our dead, but the all-important nuclear weapons. Those weapons might have provided technology which the Iranians could have used at some later date.

After returning from this operation, the Raven and I brought our families to a Fourth of July celebration at Fort Bragg. It was the first time the wives and children met and it began the lifelong relationship between our whole families as well as the two of us. I remember when, during a break in the fireworks, I asked the Raven about his military background, and he recommended I read the brilliant series called the *Brotherhood of War* by WEB Griffin and *Charlie Mike* by Leonard Scott.

It's funny how life sometimes parallels someone else's story. The Raven and the Hawk met as young Field Marshal's Lieutenants (actually we were Majors) and progressed through the ranks to eventually become a General and a Colonel.

6 CATCHING THE BAD GUYS

In October 1985, the *Achille Lauro*, an Italian cruise ship with over a thousand passengers and crew, including Americans, on board, was hijacked in the Mediterranean.

Four Palestinian terrorists were responsible for this heinous crime on the high seas. The original plan by the four terrorists was to travel to Israel to carry out an attack. A crew member spotted them in their cabin cleaning their weapons and raised the alarm, so they seized the ship.

Later, an American, the wheel-chair-bound Leon Klinghoffer, was mercilessly murdered by the cowardly terrorists and thrown overboard.

Before we knew it, the Hawk and his Air Force unit, a number of specially-modified Army helicopters and aircrews, and two Navy SEAL Assault Teams were winging their way to a little island in the Mediterranean Sea. Upon arrival, we hit the ground running and started planning our assault on the ship. We had practiced this particular operation for several years now, and it looked like a great opportunity to put our training to the test.

The plan would require a helicopter assault force to position the SEALs on the cruise ship in order to rescue the passengers from the terrorists. As we were drawing up the routes, distances and refueling requirements, word came that the terrorists had surrendered and were giving themselves up as the ship sailed into Alexandria, Egypt.

Although the situation seemed resolved and we should have been thankful, we were terribly deflated and began our preparations for redeployment. Not long after, one of the SEAL Teams was loaded up in a C-141 and immediately took off. The rest of us were traveling in an additional two C-141s, and the Hawk had been sent down to the ramp to coordinate with the aircrews for fuel loads, flight plans, and scheduled departure times for our return flight home. I received the information and headed back to the hangar where we had been biv-ouacked. As I approached, I noticed an unusual amount of activity. Battle gear was being prepared, weapons and ammo were carefully being handed out, and guys who had taken sleeping pills for the long flight back home were sticking their fingers down their throats in attempts to throw them up.

I was certainly perplexed. I came upon a very good SEAL friend of mine and asked him "What the fuck is going on?" He coolly replied, "We're going to get us some chicken, motherfuckin' rag heads!"

I had not a clue what he was talking about, but was immediately caught up in the excitement of the moment.

I ran to my Colonel, the Fox, and he told me that through intelligence sources, information that the four terrorists, who had given themselves up in Egypt, were to be flown in an Egypt Air 737 from Cairo to Tunis, Tunisia that evening. In addition, the mastermind behind the evil act, Abu Abbas, would also be on board the commercial jet. A direct order had come from Washington that our Navy SEAL assault element was to be the force of choice to capture the terrorists once they had been diverted to a ground location.

The hulking American military complex immediately went into action. An aircraft carrier, the USS Saratoga, and its accompanying battle group of destroyers, cruisers and support ships were on station in the Mediterranean at the time. When it was reported that the airplane with the terrorists aboard had departed, four of the Saratoga's F-14 Tomcats were scrambled into the air and headed off into the dark sky looking for the Egypt Air 737.

At approximately the same time, our two C-141s launched from our island base in the eastern Med and headed toward Italy. The plan was for the F-14s to intercept the 737 and force it to land at Sigonella Naval Air Station on the eastern side of the island of Sicily. Sigonella is an important and strategically located Navy support air base, but it is on Italian soil.

Remember my comment about Murphy earlier? Can you imagine the surprise of everyone in our cockpits when the F-14s initially intercepted the two C-141s streaking across the Mediterranean's dark velvet sky?

Our aircraft were ahead of the Egypt Air 737 but flying along approximately the same routes and altitudes. I had our pilots get on the radios and tell the Tomcat pilots, "Hey, we're the good guys!" When all the confusion was cleared up, the F-14s streaked away with their afterburners glowing like burning embers in the dark. Everybody had to pause for a moment, then take a quick breath of air and collect themselves. The consequences of a possible shoot-down of our two aircraft, carrying some of America's deadliest warriors, by friendlies would have been a significant tragedy of national proportion.

The Fox was seated next to our Commanding General in the belly of the C-141. The General was on a headset and talked directly to the Secretary of Defense back in Washington by satellite communications radio.

The order was plain and simple - capture the terrorists anyway we saw fit. The General passed the order to my Colonel. The Fox was on a separate headset talking to me, as I was seated up front in the cockpit talking to the two aircrews flying the C-141s. His broad guidance to the Hawk was to ensure we landed our planes right behind the 737 wherever it landed. I "Rogered" out and began to issue orders.

The young Captains sitting at the controls of the C-141s received direct guidance from a three-month pinned-on Major, not much older than them.

First, I had them dial in the frequency on one of our radios to listen to the intercept by the Tomcats of the 737. To be able to listen to the dialogue between the F-14s and the civilian pilots was simply amazing. The F-14 pilot was very blunt and in an unemotional voice stated the following, "Egypt Air 2843, this is Alpha 11. You will follow my directions or you will be shot down." It was nothing fancy, but very direct and straight to the point.

If I had been in the Egypt Air pilot's shoes right then and there, staring through the plane's windscreen at four of America's finest war machines ready to blow me out of the sky, my eyes would have been as wide as saucers and my heart would have been beating wildly. Their high-pitched and nervous response was "We understand but could you please move away from our aircraft?" The F-14s had snuggled up alongside of the 737 which positioned them within mere feet of the commercial airliner. The planes were so near each other that the commercial pilots were seriously concerned. If it was daylight, they would have had no problem reading the crew chief's name that was usually painted on the jet just under where the canopy closed. That must have been some sight, I thought at the time!

The F-14 pilot then gave directions to the civilian airliner to declare an emergency with the Italian air traffic controllers (whom we were all communicating with), and ask to land immediately at Sigonella Naval Air Station in Sicily. The Egypt Air pilot did as requested, however, he almost made a fatal mistake. He asked to land at Catania, which was a civilian airport just north of Sigonella.

The F-14 pilot had to gently remind him that he was to land at Sigonella or face the consequences.

In the meantime, as the intercept took place, I directed our two C-141s to descend and hold in two circular patterns at the end of the Sigonella runway just over the

Mediterranean waters at 6000 and 7000 feet. My plan was to await the 737 and his F-14 escorts, and as they passed us on their approach to the field, I would have the two C-141s tuck right in behind it in order to land in sequence. The first C-141 was full of SEAL assault team members and my aircraft was filled with staff, planners, medics, and radio operators.

Just as I had envisioned, we watched the 737 pass our positions with an F-14 on each wing as his escorts. As the 737 turned downwind, I directed our pilots to follow. The 737 proceeded to land and rolled to the end of the runway. At the end, the aircraft turned left on a perpendicular taxiway and stopped.

A SEAL assault team commanded by another good friend, the Night Rider, was already in place at Sigonella. They had been the first team directed to return to the US when the terrorists gave themselves up. Their aircraft was at Sigonella getting refueled for the long flight back to the States. Through our satellite communications, Night Rider was ordered to keep the aircraft from moving once it had landed and cleared the runway, which is exactly what he and his team did. One of the Night Rider's men even threw his assault gear under the aircraft's tires to prevent it from taxiing.

As our C-141s were on short final, the Italian aircraft controllers screamed over the radios, "American aircraft, go around! Go around! Go around!" They did not want us to land. They also began to turn the runway lights alternately to full bright and then completely off.

I believe they really meant what they said but I had my

orders. I told both aircraft's pilots to disregard the tower's instructions and land their planes as I directed. Those pilots, disciplined military airmen, did as I requested and landed on the runway approximately one minute apart, rolled out to the end and came to a full stop right behind the 737.

As the first C-141 came to a halt, the crew entrance door flew open and disgorged a firestorm of activity. It was like somebody kicking over a red ant pile. Navy SEALs, dressed all in black, carrying MP-5 assault weapons, CAR-15s and 203-MM rocket launchers immediately surrounded the 737 and linked up with Night Rider's assault team. From every imaginable position and angle, the aircraft was completely under surveillance and totally secured within seconds.

As the passenger door entrance on the 737 opened and a crewmember stuck his head out, an eerie laser light show commenced. Every operator had a red laser beam pointer attached to his weapon, which would allow him to sight his weapon in total darkness in the flash of an instant. More than thirty beams were centered on the middle of the forehead and chest of this poor aircrew member. Seeing all the red dots slow dancing on his body, he immediately ducked back inside.

As I rushed out of the second aircraft to witness this phenomenal sequence of events, the whole air base began to come alive. This was all happening about midnight and there was usually not too much activity going on at this time of night at the airfield. Very quickly, the ant pile began to expand.

Airport fire trucks and rescue vehicles, emergency lights flashing and adding color to the bright spectacle, hustled out of their garages and immediately drove onto the runway. The drivers then parked their vehicles behind the stopped C-141s, effectively blocking the aircraft from turning around and taking off in the opposite direction.

About 600 Carabinieri personnel (the Italian police) then arrived in all manner of police cars and emergency vehicles with their flashing lights on, surrounding our positions. It became the proverbial Mexican standoff.

As this was unfolding, Abu Abbas happened to look out the aircraft passenger door one time to see what all the commotion was about. A Navy SEAL sharpshooter immediately sighted his red dot from his long-range sniper rifle on Abbas's head. Only the many years of good order and discipline prevented him from squeezing the trigger and ridding this world of one of its worst terrorist masterminds.

Following orders from Washington, our mission had become clearer. We were to give the terrorists over to the Italians and leave. The ship that had been hijacked was Italian and although an American had been killed, we would do the righteous and morally correct thing.

Our Commanding General made contact with the senior officer commanding the Italian force that was surrounding us. He told him we were to escort the terrorists off the plane and hand them over to the Italian authorities for jurisdiction.

We then received another request over our satellite radio. Another C-141 was being flown to Cairo, Egypt, and would pickup the newly widowed Mrs. Klinghoffer. She would be flown to our location at the air base in Italy. We requested that a criminal-type police lineup be established which would allow Mrs. Klinghoffer the opportunity to pick out the terrorists. These conditions were agreed to and the next day we were allowed to taxi our C-141s off the runway, the fire trucks were removed and the C-141 with Mrs. Klinghoffer was allowed to land.

Our Commanding General met the aircraft, escorted Mrs. Klinghoffer to the brig (this was a Navy base, after all) and began the process of identifying the bad guys. As she walked down the line, Mrs. Klinghoffer identified each terrorist in a rather dramatic fashion. She looked at the individuals whom she knew had hijacked her and her husband's dreams, painfully staring into their faces and stated, "I spit on you." Upon completion of the identification process by Mrs. Klinghoffer, our two C-141s were allowed to depart the airfield.

The police lineup actually occurred the next evening after the initial aircraft intercept, when another intelligence source gave us some startling information. We found out that the Italians had safely taken Abu Abbas off the 737 and escorted him to Catania airport. The Italians were then putting him on a commercial flight to Rome.

One of our staff guys, known as Mad Dog, was quick to take action. With the runway blocked by fire trucks, he commandeered a Navy T-39 and had the pilots take off on the taxiway and take him to Rome. We were not about to let Abbas get away! Unfortunately, when Abbas got to Rome, the Italians quickly put him on a flight to

Yugoslavia and from there he made his way to Iraq and went into hiding.

Only recently, after the invasion of Iraq did the United States finally capture Abu Abbas. He was caught in Baghdad by American Special Forces in April 2003. In recent years Abbas lived in Iraq under the protection of Saddam Hussein.

Abbas, whose real name was Muhammad Abbas, faced a life sentence in Italy after being convicted *in absentia* in 1986 for the Klinghoffer murder. In March 2004, Abbas died in a prison outside of Baghdad at the age of 55 from a heart attack. His legal status was being debated by US authorities at the time of his death. American officials were considering prosecuting him in the United States or turning him over to the Italian government or elsewhere. Almost 19 years later we finally caught the big fish who thought he got away, proving again the old adage, "You can run, but you can't hide." The United States of America will eventually get you.

At the time of the Abbas capture, Raven held a very high position in the Special Operations command structure and was instrumental in making this happen.

Early the next morning, after Mrs. Klinghoffer completed the identification process, we cranked our Starlifter's big jet engines and began our journey back to America. What an incredible sense of accomplishment and satisfaction we felt. We had just conducted one of the most daring and audacious missions I have ever had the honor to be a part of. You cannot imagine the adrenaline high we had been on for those six days. No sleep and your mind spinning, the war stories all started to flow. There was much laughter and joy on all the faces as I looked around the cavernous interior of the aircraft. We were America's newest darlings and yet nobody knew who we were and what we had done. What a gas!

Although the Raven was not a participant of this particular mission, we had met many challenges in life by this time, but I had yet to meet the specter of personal death. I had been exposed to death, I had delivered death to others, but, unlike the Raven, I had yet to experience the all-consuming sense of mortality that real closeness to personal death brings, the experience that had born Raven's own demons. That was about to change.

7 TURKEY LEG

As I made my final descent, I looked down, and the four wires were right below me. It appeared like I was going to land between the middle two. There was no time to bend over and "kiss my ass goodbye" or even have my life flash by. I just knew that I had fucked up and I was in big trouble!

A small window of opportunity opened for the Hawk to soar with the Eagles. A slot to Accelerated Free Fall (AFF) School was made available to the Hawk in order to be qualified to deploy as part of an assault command post (CP). At the completion of the school, the Hawk would be a High Altitude Low Opening (HALO) qualified "Sky God".

This training occurred in the Arizona desert and lasted all of one week. Day One, we reviewed emergency procedures and learned how to pack a parachute. Day Two found the Hawk in the back of a Cessna Caravan (a single engine turboprop aircraft) with two Navy SEALs. After climbing to 13,000 feet, we prepared to exit. I had one SEAL on each side of me. As we counted, we rocked back and forth and dove out on the count of three. I was jumping whether I wanted to or not.

This was not the time to have second thoughts and back out. The SEALs had my arms pretty well secured in their grips and were going to drag me out kicking and screaming, even if I wanted to quit right then and there.

This is an amazing milestone in one's professional life. When you exit the aircraft and plunge towards the Earth at an initial speed of 32 feet per second, you have to make a concerted effort to find your ripcord, pull it and hope for the best (a good parachute over your head) or you could wind up hurtling to your death, like a squashed jelly donut on good ol' Mother Earth.

This jump was made in the bright early morning sun, yet I have always called them night jumps because I jumped out with my eyes closed. Every time I jumped was a scary moment, and if somebody tells you they are not a little bit afraid when they jump, they're either crazy or lying.

My heart was pounding a mile a minute, and up to the moment I jumped out of the aircraft, I was praying that everything would go all right. The adrenaline rush was so overpowering when the jump was completed. You settle back on terra firma with a nice standup landing `a la the Army's Golden Knights, that for an instant, you think you have become one too.

I usually let out a small victory cry like "Oh yeah!" or "All right!" and raised my arms in victory like a boxer who has just knocked out an opponent and instantly celebrates.

When all the guys get back together at the turn in point where we hand in our parachutes to the parachute packers, we all give each other high fives and pats on the back. It is a very macho feeling, but instead of getting naked in the woods and howling at the moon, we all jumped together. That was one thing I did have in common with the Raven. We were both HALO-qualified and we have jumped together.

The fact that I became HALO-qualified amazed me when I would observe the reaction of Army personnel at Fort Bragg when they saw my uniform. I had pilot wings, Basic Airborne wings and HALO wings. The Army soldiers focused in on those HALO wings and really thought I was the cat's meow for having them, but I had a different perspective. It took almost one year of my life to earn my pilot wings and only a week to get the HALO wings. Army soldiers have a different outlook on things.

I worked for a two-star general, who told me that he liked being around people who jumped because he felt they were a "different breed of cat." He thought there was something in the makeup of any individual who had the moxie to jump out of a perfectly safe aircraft, and he built his career by serving in several airborne units. One of the units he spent much of his military career in was the 82nd Airborne Division, a group whose whole way of life is built around airborne operations and parachuting. From the amount of time I have spent with jumpers, I found the same to be true.

I had worked around individuals like the Raven for some time, and they were special. I can hardly explain or put into words what it is like to jump out of an aircraft, link up with a SEAL and a Special Forces soldier in the air for a three-way, part and fly away, open your chute and then get back on the ground to link up again and recount the jump you just completed. It is an exhilarating experience which only those who have accomplished it can truly know or understand. It is almost better than sex.

Why am I telling you all this? Well, it happened on my thirteenth jump.

I had just completed the AFF course in Arizona. The whole damned state is a drop zone (DZ). I only made a total of twelve jumps, but was proficient enough to be signed off as qualified. I made a back-flip in the air and even felt comfortable to try that. On my fifth jump I was able to maneuver myself in the air in order to land in the Ps. The Ps is a circular pit made of gravel that was a target to land in on the ground. It was maybe twenty feet in diameter, but after jumping from almost three miles high and steering your chute properly, landing in the Ps was quite an accomplishment. The Hawk was able to do it on his fifth jump.

Somebody must have actually thought I knew what I was doing. After being signed off as qualified, I received my blood wings at a small graduation ceremony on the drop zone. A Navy SEAL, named Carl Keith, slammed the two gold points on the back of Navy jump wings into my chest with his fist, drawing blood! I felt like I had become a member of a special circle of men. It was my final initiation into a select breed of people.

Well, back to jump number thirteen. I had just returned to North Carolina and the Command was having a proficiency jump. We normally had two jump operations a month to maintain proficiency and for this, we received a whopping $110.00 extra a month jump pay. You had to jump once every three months to get the pay and with all the traveling, conferences and meetings, you were lucky to jump maybe once a month or even once every two months. The day before my fateful incident, an avid jumper from the unit, who was the Executive Officer (XO) at the time, came to see me in my office. He said the unit was going to make a jump the next day at a small airfield in eastern North Carolina. The Command rented a Beechcraft Twin Bonanza, which could haul five jumpers at a time, and we had fifteen slots for guys going to jump. The XO thought this would be the perfect opportunity to get my first jump with the unit since graduating from AFF.

We drove over to this airfield on a crisp, cold December morning eight days before Christmas and conducted our jump briefing. Five of us (including me) were quickly stuffed into the Bonanza. My jumpmaster was a guy we called "the Thumb" because he had one that was extremely large. There was also a Navy SEAL jumping with me who arranged the slot at AFF for me and was a very close personal friend. The DZ was a little open field next to the runway we took off from. In just a few minutes, I would realize just how little the DZ was.

We climbed to 10,000 feet and jumped out. I was

number four in the stick and remembered watching as the Thumb blasted by me in the Delta position (arms at his sides and head diving toward the ground).

Now remember, I was only on jump number thirteen. I am an experienced pilot, and knew that you fly a square parachute just like an airplane making an approach to land. There is a downwind leg, a turn to a crosswind leg, then a turn to final, and land heading into the wind.

The winds were rather high this morning, but I didn't realize how high. I was trying to stick to the basics. I had an altimeter on my wrist that constantly showed my altitude. My training said I was supposed to be at 1500 feet on downwind, 800-1000 feet on crosswind and turn final at 500 feet. So, as I concentrated on my altitudes, I was not aware of my ground speed. The winds were up to about twenty knots, and the chute, on a no-wind day, flies at 22 knots. Therefore, when I was downwind, I was smoking along the ground at over 40 knots (wind plus chute speed). When I turned final, I was only going two knots forward speed (chute speed minus wind). I had made a terrible miscalculation in the air and would soon realize it.

When I turned final and was pointed at the DZ, I was over a forest of 40-foot tall pine trees. As I was drifting agonizingly slow toward the little field, it quickly became apparent I was in deep trouble. As I got closer, there was a paved asphalt road with T-shaped telephone poles alongside that were between the 40-foot pine trees and the DZ. Draped over these telephone poles were four one-inch-thick steel-braided cables about thirty feet high.

My choices were three. First, I could turn around and fly into the trees at forty miles an hour and probably impale myself on a tree branch. Second, I could try to make a ninety-degree turn and land on the road and maybe get run over by a car, or hit the ground so hard I might injure myself severely or even kill myself (which actually happened to another jumper a couple of years later). Or third, I could attempt to make it over the wires and land on the DZ. I went for the last option.

To try and explain it, unless you were there, is extremely difficult. This all happened so very fast and I was trying to gauge the situation, digest all the inputs into my brain from exterior sources and come up with the right decision.

I did not come up with the perfect solution. My margin of error was very close but missed by about six to 12 inches.

What happened next I can only relay from what guys on the ground saw and what I felt. People who were watching said I reflexively bent my legs back hoping I would miss the lines. Unfortunately, my left knee and left foot momentarily brushed the last two lines. The instant I hit the lines, I felt incredible pain.

We've all been shocked before but this was way beyond that. I was shocked to the nth degree. The pain was so intense that I remember the world looked as if it was spinning out of control. Like when you are in a drunken stupor, and you lay down in bed, and you get the "spins", was what my eyes were doing. I didn't get knocked out, but my vision was totally distorted.

The guys on the ground waiting to go up for the next drop, said that when I hit the wires a large flash and bang like a lightning bolt with thunder was all they saw. They were immediately convinced that I was a dead man.

I then fell approximately thirty feet to the ground. The chute continued to somewhat fly me to the ground, and the other jumpers said it looked like I then conducted a poor Parachute Landing Fall (PLF). A PLF is where you touch the balls of your feet, lean to one side and then hit your calf, buttock and push-up muscle in that order. Actually, I was like a drunk in a car wreck and was not in control of my body at the time.

When I hit the ground, the guys said, I hit like a "sack of shit." My body was really loose and the landing momentarily knocked the wind out of me. I do remember going "Ugh" as I hit and my eyes immediately refocused and I instantly knew where I was. I ended up lying on my back with my legs crossed, sort of propped up by my reserve parachute. I looked down at my legs and smoke was pouring from them. The pain was brutal now.

The electrical shock blew a small hole in the top of my left boot where my big toe was. It also melted my jumpsuit to the side of my left knee where I made the momentary contact with the power lines.

The guys on the ground ran to where I was lying to check on my condition. My Navy SEAL friend, who had jumped with me, landed on the drop zone with no problem and was getting out of his chute when I hit the lines. He immediately dropped his gear and ran over to me. His face is the only one I remember.

He knelt down beside me, and I looked up at him and told him "I'm hurt." He looked at my smoking legs and said something like everything is going to be all right and that I was fine. I had just hit some serious power lines and this guy was telling me I'm OK. You know what? I believed him. Yeah, I was in extreme pain at that moment but this guy, whom I would have trusted with my life, was telling me everything was going to be A-OK. I needed that, because I was really one fucked-up dude right then.

I couldn't move my body from the waist down, and I was asking people to pull my legs up. I thought that the electricity had shocked my muscles so severely that they were super-intensified into a pulling motion, trying to draw my legs up into a fetal position. With my legs stretched out and my being unable to move them, I thought if somebody pulled my legs up to a bent position, it would relieve some of the pain I was feeling.

The guys wouldn't move my legs as I requested because I couldn't move my legs by myself. They all thought I might have broken my back in the final fall to the ground, or I had damaged my spine and become paralyzed. Therefore, they brought out a backboard from an emergency ambulance parked nearby, placed me on it and immobilized my entire body and head with restraining straps. Then they made a radio call for an emergency medical evacuation. An Army helicopter launched from the nearby Fort Bragg Simmons Army Airfield and came to retrieve the broken Hawk.

I do remember feeling quite scared also and I asked my Navy SEAL friend to go with me to the hospital. He said "No problem", jumped into the helo, and held my hand the entire time, from the minute we left the ground until we were in the emergency room at Womack Army Hospital.

You watch TV and see that scene played over and over again in a situation where somebody is close to death, and a friend holds their hand or cradles their head and provides comfort and support.

Well, that really happened to the Hawk and this giant Navy SEAL was the guy holding this poor little scrawny Air Force pilot's hand during my hour of greatest need. I honestly and truly believe that was one of the most critical points in my recovery. I will forever remember and always be grateful to that selfless Navy SEAL for being there to hold my hand. I have always thought it must be something close to being in combat, getting seriously shot and having your best buddy be at your side to bandage you up and carry you to safety.

When I got to the hospital, the doctors from our unit swarmed all over me. They cut off my jump suit, wrapped me in blankets to keep me from going into shock, and injected me with painkillers. My left leg had swollen up above the knee, and the doctors thought they might have to operate immediately, because there was a possibility blood might not be flowing down through my leg. However, within minutes, I could start to move my toes on the left foot, which was a good sign.

They decided that I did have circulation and would not operate. I was then sent to the Intensive Care Unit (ICU) and given twenty-four-hour around-the-clock care and observation. This lasted for three days.

I had an EKG taken which showed my heart beating a little irregularly, because of the electrical charge my body had took. People have asked me how much of an electrical charge I had taken, and to this day, I still don't know and don't really care. All I know is that it was a lot more than I ever wanted, and I was very lucky to still be alive. The electricity could have traveled up my legs to my heart or further on to my head and blown out the top. It could have blown off one of my legs or some other extremity. What it actually did was jump to my other leg, in the right front shin and out the back through three holes behind my right knee.

A catheter was inserted, which was about as painful as the electrical shock. I had to have this contraption put in so that I could urinate and the medical personnel could take samples. My first urine was totally brown. This indicated that I had burned muscle, which was absorbed into the blood. Blood is a purifier for the body and takes away the bad stuff, so this was actually a good sign.

On the third day, I was moved out of ICU and placed in a private hospital room. A pretty young nurse came in with two crutches and said it was time for me to walk. I said, "You've got to be kidding!" but the look on her face was totally serious. The quicker you get the patient moving the better chance for recovery she told me.

Beads of sweat broke out on my forehead, and I almost passed out as I struggled down the hallway on my crutches. It was another new pain sensation, one of many, which would continue for well over two years. I was as white as a sheet when I finished my ten-minute stroll down the hospital corridor, but the hospital staff said I did great, which I guess was supposed to make up for the pain.

Then a completely different type of pain was put on my agenda. I had to go to physical therapy every morning, sit in a whirl pool and have my burned legs scrubbed with a steel brush to rid my body of dead and potentially infectious tissue. This required me to take a shot of Demerol before the treatment started.

Don't let anybody kid you - this did not remove or greatly deaden the pain. It might have made it a little bit more tolerable, but it still hurt like hell.

I was released from the hospital on the sixth day, two days before Christmas, but only with the promise that I would continue to return every morning for my special bath at physical therapy.

Jerry T. and Sophia were the Hawk's physical therapists. He was a methodical man about his business, and she was kind and gentle. He took great pride in his work and scrubbed really hard. She was worried about how to keep my skin the same color, and would rub aloe lotion on the burned areas. I didn't think scrubbing dead skin off people would be a terrific job, but ten years later I personally went to see them and thank them for their service, although at the time I didn't appreciate it. They were the "somebodies doing the something" whom you take for granted or whose importance you don't realize until you really need them. They were, indeed, another piece of the great puzzle of life. Jerry and Sofia were part of all the King's horses and all the King's men (and women) that put the Hawk together again.

On Christmas Day, while my family attended church, I was at home in bed watching television and the movie

It's a Wonderful Life came on. As Jimmy Stewart's character, George, plunged to the depths of despair, and he
prepared to jump off a bridge, I could easily relate to his
emotional state of mind. I remember my family returning home and seeing me cry like a little baby as my spirits
sank to an all-time low on this Christmas Day. It was only
when Clarence, the guardian angel, saved George that my
tears turned from ones of helplessness to ones of hope.

On New Year's Day, my wife and I were invited to a
party at Taffy's house. Taffy was a soldier in the Raven's
unit. It had been 15 days since my accident, and I was
still feeling pretty low. I felt I needed to get out of the
house and be around my co-workers in order to help my
mental state.

Going to the party and hobbling in on crutches, I was
greeted warmly by everyone in attendance. The Raven
was at the party and we sat outside. I explained to him
how my accident unfolded. After I completed telling my
story, the Raven told me that the same thing had almost
happened to him on a jump. His exception was that he
had almost hit the power lines. His power lines though
were the ones that run between the giant towers you always see Godzilla stomping on in those Japanese sci-fi
flicks, and it was at night.

Here was a man I greatly admired, admitting that he
had made a near-fatal error as well. It seems like the old
axiom is true, that "There are those who have been hurt
in jump accidents and those who will be hurt."

He then told me that I was more than welcome to
come down to his facility for my rehabilitation training.

The Raven's compound was a state-of-the- art, multimillion-dollar complex covering a couple of acres. From the outside it looked like a Red Roof Inn, which gave the place one of its nicknames. We also called it Wally World after that Chevy Chase movie in which the Griswolds travel across America to Wally World only to find it closed.

This was Raven's unit's world-class training facility and only people with special access could get in. Within the compound were an Olympic-sized swimming pool and a multi-man hydrotherapeutic pool.

Being invited to go whenever I wanted and to be welcomed into this closed world was something I will always treasure from the Raven. This open invitation is one of those small miracles that give you the motivation to go on and fight the good fight.

After my operations, I would drive the twenty minutes to the Raven's place and start to swim laps, followed by a dip in the giant hot tub. That was my small joke. I always called the hydrotherapeutic pool a hot tub, and that pissed the Raven off. The pool was justified in the building of the facility as a necessary piece of equipment for rehabilitation purposes and I called it a hot tub. Sometimes I can be a schmuck.

In early January, I was scheduled for debridement surgery. The skin had finally died down to the bone, and it coagulated into a blackish-looking leathery piece on the side of my left leg where I touched the wire. The doctor said he needed to operate and remove this leathery piece surgically.

I was put back into the hospital for five days to have the surgery and some recovery time. When I awoke and the pain medication started to wear off, I went into another level of pain toleration. When the wrappings came off and I was able to inspect the surgery, I looked down and saw this oval 4 by 6 inch hole in my leg. It stretched from the top left side of my knee and extended six inches halfway down my calf. The middle of the hole was opened right down to the bone, so I was looking at my exposed left fibula. About an inch of the outside portion of the oval was angry red, exposed bloody skin. I had a picture taken of it, and when somebody looked at the picture, they commented that it looked like something from a triage-training scenario; it didn't look real. It was more like a dummy's leg surgically dressed up to appear like it had a serious leg wound.

The doctor said the electricity had killed everything that I was looking at, and he had made the best of a bad situation. He had to expose the underneath portion of my skin in order to begin the healing process. The next part of this process was another "shoot to the moon" kind of pain, because I was sent home for two weeks and had to have the dressing changed twice a day.

This was an incredibly depressing experience. Large portions of gauze were placed over the open wound, and then adhesive tape would encircle the leg to keep the gauze in place. By the time twelve hours passed, blood and other life fluids had oozed out of the bloody red skin and coagulated into the gauze. I dropped from 158 pounds down to 143 pounds in two weeks time. Dropping so much weight off an already slender build, one can imagine how thin I looked. I was very pale and looked like somebody from a refugee camp that was reduced to just skin and bones.

I would pop two Percocets (heavy duty painkillers) twenty minutes prior to the changing of the dressing to help fight the ensuing pain. The process was like the changing of the guard. All the pieces were laid out on a nightstand next to my bed: new gauze, a roll of adhesive tape, Keri lotion, a tube of zinc oxide and a couple of bottles of saline solution. A large piece of hospital bed covering was put under my leg and the process began. My wife would pour some saline solution onto the gauze in order to loosen it somewhat from its dried coagulated state. The saline solution was used to prevent possible infections to an exposed wound. I would begin to peel off the gauze ever so slowly and scream or come close to passing out as the gauze being pulled away was tormenting the nerve endings of my skin.

My wife and children kept telling me to shut up and quit acting like a crybaby. They were pretty tough on me, but this probably helped with my recovery. I would get very mad at them and try to prove that I could withstand the pain. This process would last for some time, as the throbbing pain would ebb to an acceptable level so that I could pull some more of the gauze away. I was doing it by small increments. It was more like pulling a piece of adhesive tape off your arm and ripping the hairs off in one fell swoop, but continuing to do it over and over again.

After the gauze was finally off, my daughter put Keri lotion on the surrounding skin that was not burned as badly, but still needed some type of treatment. Then zinc oxide was applied to the worst burned areas and the gauze was then reapplied over the hole and taped to my leg. Twelve hours later the process would start all over again.

One time, early in the morning, as I was hobbling to the bathroom, I glanced down at my right leg, and saw blood oozing through the gauze. I fell to the floor, unwrapped the gauze, and looked, horrified, at my leg. My right shin had a burned area that exposed a vein running down the front of my leg. Somehow the vein split open, and blood was gushing out of the opening. I sat on the hallway floor and started to call my wife's name in a pleading, whiney kind of voice. She came running from the bedroom, looked at me, and took action. She applied pressure until the blood coagulated and the bleeding stopped. I thought I was going to bleed to death. It was just another small setback in this hell-on-earth adventure.

When I completed initial static-line jump school the year before, I thought of the movie *Apocalypse Now* and the role of Colonel Kurtz played by Marlon Brando. Before he became a rebel leader, hiding in the jungle with his own renegade army, the guy sent to terminate him (with prejudice) was reading his file. In the file, it said that Kurtz had gone to jump school late in his Army career at the age of 38. That is an accurate assessment. I would say 99 per cent of all personnel, regardless of service, who go to jump school, do so when they are in their teens or early twenties. I was 36 at the time of static line training and 38 by the time I finished AFF.

I thought I was invincible and some kind of super-human, special warrior. I was wrong again, which seemed to happen fairly often in my life. In retrospect, whatever strength and mysterious power I thought I had or feeling of being invincible actually transferred to my wife. As I became the weaker one, she became stronger. As I lost faith or complained about how unfair life was, my wife took the family and me under her wing and became the special warrior. She knew I was hurting, but never let it show. She came up with hare-brained schemes to keep my spirits up. The one I remember most vividly she hatched up with one of my best friends from pilot training.

One day, as I was lying on the couch watching, but not watching, some afternoon television show, which could have been some silly soap opera or a rerun of the *Rockford Files*, the telephone rang. She answered the phone and said, "It's for you." We had a cordless phone and she brought it to me while I was lying on the couch. I took the phone, said my name and asked politely to whom I was speaking. The answer I received was astonishing. My friend had disguised his voice and proceeded to tell me he was a representative of the Publisher's Clearinghouse company. He said I had just been randomly selected and was a winner of their million dollar sweepstakes, which was so popular at the time. This was the television ad seen all the time, with Johnny Carson's sidekick, Ed McMahon from *The Tonight Show*, telling America about the latest winner.

Well, I was being told I was this person, and he had me going hook, line and sinker. I was saying, "You gotta be kidding me", "I can't believe it" and so on and so forth. He kept asking me all these official sounding questions, acting like he needed information. I was completely fooled, until he broke down and started to laugh after a few minutes. After I knew who it was, I looked over and there was my wife smiling sheepishly. I found out from my friend that she had called him and asked him to help her cheer me up. I had been pretty down in the dumps, and she thought I needed a real hearty laugh. Well, I roared out loud, but my anger was totally in jest as I was caught up in the moment. I told them both I was going to kill them whenever I got my strength back. I believe that was what eventually happened. For a long time my wife was the strength of our family, but she transferred the power back as I got healthier and stronger, and I will be forever thankful and grateful to her.

During this time, I would go to the doctor's office for consultations about the next step in the recovery process. He explained that I had two options. First, he could commence grafting small portions of skin onto the bloody exposed part and slowly fill in the hole. I asked him how long this would take, and he replied about two years. I then asked what the second option was. He calmly explained in great detail about something he called a gastroc flap.

Initially, he would fillet open my leg from the bottom of the oval hole to just above my left ankle and rip out one of my two calf muscles (shit, I didn't even know I had two). Actually, he said he would snip the bottom part of the muscle and transfer the entire muscle onto the top of the hole in my leg. He would then pile the muscle up like a plate of spaghetti and staple it in place. After this, he would thinly slice some skin from my ass and hip to use as grafts and place them on top of the muscle.

A muscle has its own blood supply, and the skin needs this blood to thrive and grow. The grafts would have to be put through a contraption that looked a little bit like a meat grinder. It cut these small, diamond-shaped holes into the skin grafts that would allow them to be stretched out and cover the larger wound opening. If the graft took properly, the skin would grow and fill in the missing little diamond shapes.

I asked how long this procedure would take. He said the operation and initial recovery time would take a little over a week, if everything took the first time. With physical therapy, I could be operational in six months. I asked what the odds were, and he said a 20 percent chance if everything went perfectly. Now, the doctor who explained this operation to me had me a little worried when I first met him. He would sometimes show up wearing two different sneakers, a big cowlick of hair sticking up out of his head, and little pieces of toilet paper stuck to his face from where he nicked it shaving that morning. This did not instill a lot of confidence in me until I found out something about his background.

This guy graduated from West Point and went directly into the infantry. He was a rifle platoon leader in the 82nd Airborne Division at Fort Bragg for six years before he decided he was tired of slogging through the mud and living in the field. He applied for medical school, was accepted, and the Army sent him to the Eisenhower Medical School for four years. He graduated in the top two percent in the country and was sent back to Fort Bragg to complete his internship at Womack Army Medical Center.

I was one of his first patients and he later told me I became one of his star patients and success stories. I became as proud of him as he, perhaps, became of me. We were a team and went through this very difficult process together for many months. He actually took pictures of my wounds and his treatments and put them in a scrapbook.

He told me sometimes medicine is not a science, and he couldn't answer all my questions. He would be as honest as possible and try to explain the surgical procedure in laymen's terms so this dumb Air Force pilot might understand. I told him I would get back to him after I made some inquiries. I called my sister who was a nurse and she told me about an individual who had been severely injured in a motorcycle accident. He'd had the same type of operation I was being offered, and it worked on him. She said the human body can do amazing things, and I believed her. So, I went back to the Doc and told him to "Go for it." I wanted to go for the whole enchilada. "Damn the torpedoes, full speed ahead", I said.

Finally, in late January 1988, the surgery was scheduled, and the operation required four doctors. I needed an orthopedic surgeon to shave off the burned portion of the bone in my leg. That was another part I was unaware of. I didn't know I had electrocuted my leg bone also and part of it had to be removed. My doctor would then slice my leg open and do the transfer of the calf muscle while being observed and guided by a doctor from Duke University Medical School, who specialized in this type of surgery.

My doctor said this was the first time he was going to do this type of surgery, and he wanted an expert around to help him. I didn't argue with that logic. The fourth doctor was an intern from Duke who would sew the hole on top of my left big toe together. I was put to sleep for the operation but I could visualize these doctors hovering around me, probably making jokes and planning on how much money to put into which mutual fund or stock. To me this was some serious stuff and not FM (fucking magic).

I would like to have ended this chapter here with a happy ending, but that didn't happen. After coming out of surgery I was put back in the ICU for recovery time. In the middle of the night, I abruptly awoke as the painkillers from the operation started to wear off, and this new pain took me to bigger and greater heights. I guess, after this kind of radical surgery, which involved moving so many parts around, my body was reacting quite negatively. I called for the nurse, and she gave me a shot of morphine. This still didn't help because the severity of the pain was so intense. She then called an anesthesiologist, who started an intravenous drip of a numbing agent into my lower back. It was supposed to completely numb me from the waist down. He did such a good job that he actually gave me too much numbing agent. This was about 3:00 a.m. and he must have been a little sleepy. He left and went home, and I remember lying in bed, actually sensing the numbing agent moving slowly up my body.

As it started to near my heart, I freaked. I was thinking that the stuff will get to my heart and make it stop beating or up to my brain and make it stop functioning. I began to hallucinate and watched the Grim Reaper enter my room, and he was walking towards me. He was dressed in a black robe with bony hands extended from his sleeves as he reached for me. I made the most foolish plea to God, that if he would only save me, I would never do another thing wrong in my life again. I frantically pushed the button next to my bed that would ring down at the nurse's station and summon her to my plight. As she walked in, I pleaded with her to turn off the numbing agent that was seeping into my veins. She said she was not authorized, and I told her to call the anesthesiologist back to work immediately.

She looked at me kind of strangely, but she must have been convinced by the way I acted that something was wrong. She called the anesthesiologist and he told her how to turn off the drip. By the time he got dressed and drove to the ICU, I was virtually hyperventilating. I explained my sensations and he gave me a shot of Valium to calm me down, which immediately knocked me out. The next thing I knew, I woke up and felt that damned numbing agent heading up my body again. The guy had restarted the agent drip while I was out cold and had left to go home again.

I immediately summoned the nurse again and told her to take the intravenous feed out of me, and I would deal with the pain. She said she couldn't without authorization. I screamed back at her "Fuck the authorization.

I'm giving you the fucking authorization. You need to stop that fucking agent from coming into my body or I'll pull that motherfucker out myself!" She acquiesced and pulled the plug.

I don't know if she called that anesthesiologist back, but early the next morning, my doctor showed up and I explained to him the situation as I saw it. I told him no more numbing agents. He said okay, and I then started getting shots of Demerol every four hours. They hardly worked, but at least I didn't think I was dying.

A few days later, the next bit of bad news hit me. Before I went into the operation, everything was actually in working order. I could walk on my own and flex all my moving parts. During the operation, my peroneal nerve, which controls foot movement, was somehow bruised and damaged. Lying in bed, I could not pull my left foot backwards. My mind said move, but the foot would just lie there. It is very frustrating to think about something that you take for granted one moment and in the next, have it taken away from you. I had what was called "dropped foot."

When I told my doctor, he didn't seem too distressed. I am not sure if he was trying to hide his disappointment that the operation was not a complete success by not showing any concern at the time. I assumed it was part of the surgery and that it would quickly heal and the motor movement would return. I was way wrong!

Five days after the surgery, the big day arrived. It was time to take off the dressings and look at the leg. It seemed like a cast of thousands was in my room that day.

Nurses, doctors, and lookie-loos were all in there.

When the final piece of gauze was removed, I stared at this bluish, purplish oozing lump of meat sticking out of the side of my leg. To me, it looked like a Cornish game hen that had been plucked of its feathers, impacted into the side of my leg and somehow gotten stuck there! Others looked at it and remarked how it looked just like turkey skin. I said "My God, what is it?" and the doctors and nurses were all going "ooooh" and "ahhhh." They all said it was beautiful. I didn't understand until my doctor explained that the grafts had actually taken and this was all a healthy-looking condition.

Four more days passed before I was discharged from the hospital. I went home and was told to start my rehabilitation. Fortunately, the Command was totally supportive of my efforts to get well again; consequently, my job morphed into an hour at the office and the rest of the day at the gym. I still had the dropped foot, but they gave me a foot brace that slipped into my boot or shoe and kept my foot at a ninety-degree angle. If I didn't wear it, I could be heard walking down the hallway, since my foot slapped the floor like a horse counting numbers. I would have to throw the foot forward in order to walk somewhat correctly. I could actually push down on the foot, but I just couldn't lift it.

I started a daily regimen of intense, three-hour workouts of heavy weightlifting to get myself back in shape. My goal was to get back on parachute duty and flight status.

There were two other guys who were going through rehab at the same time who had both been in jump accidents. One guy had his knee banged up pretty badly, but the other had almost as appalling an injury as mine. He had collided with another jumper at night. The speed at which they collided at must have exceeded 130 miles per hour. Either the other jumper's equipment or his knee hit this guy's head, which knocked him out and he fell unconscious toward the ground. His automatic opening device (AOD) deployed his 'chute and saved his life. When his teammates got to him, his head was the size of a large pumpkin. I later saw a picture of him with this over-inflated head and couldn't believe it was the same person. They had to perform a tracheotomy so he could breathe, and during his rehab he had this little plastic piece sticking out of his neck that would whistle when he breathed. He would have to cover it with his hand to talk and his voice sounded something like Darth Vader. I thought he was truly courageous, and both guys were an integral factor in my recovery, as we would push each other physically in the gym. Thanks, Rod and Scotty.

I asked my doctor how much physical training I should do, and he told me that he couldn't give me a number of repetitions or sets. He did give me some of the wisest guidance I have ever received, though, which I still use to this day. He said, "Your body will tell you what you can do and how far you can push it."

The Army doctors in the hospital were a little bit confounded. They kept telling me that soldiers with lesser injuries than mine were getting out of the service, and here I was, actually trying to stay in. I can't really explain why I wanted to stay in, but my focus at the time was to get back on the horse that almost killed me.

I also started running every day. First a quarter-mile, then a half-mile, then three-quarters of a mile and so on, until finally, I could run around the airfield at Pope AFB, a distance of about six miles. I had my friend, the Critter, run with me for inspiration and spirit. He was a great runner, but would run alongside me at my ant-crawl pace so that I wouldn't quit. I kept telling him I couldn't make it, and he would give me a response like "Sure you can, or I will put a bullet in you and put you out of your misery!" Inspiration like that always helped me to keep putting one foot in front of the other!

Sometimes I felt like I could opt for the bullet, but six months and nine days after my accident I was surrounded by 10 other jumpers in the back of a C-130 flying at twelve thousand feet. I remember thinking, when we were told to stand up and move to the rear ramp, "This will all be over very shortly." To maneuver to our exit point, jump off the ramp, add the free-fall time, the under-canopy time and then land back on sweet Mother Earth, it would be less than five minutes' total time. I also knew I couldn't back out, as I was completely surrounded and had many hands holding onto my arms to drag me out if I had second thoughts. To add more tension to the moment, the jumpmaster cancelled the first two passes due to misalignment with the drop zone. By the time I stood up and was in the middle of the pack for the third pass, my heart was beating like a jackhammer and felt like it was going to explode out of my chest.

Finally, on the third pass, the jumpmaster said "Go!"

and out I went. I was getting into a nice stable position, not trying anything fancy, when all of sudden one of the jumpers came out of nowhere and positioned himself nose-to-nose with me. He reached out with his thumb and forefinger, tweaked my nose, gave me a big shit-eating grin, spun away and flew off. It sure helped break some of the tension. Thanks, Eric.

My last thought of this particular jump was the wind. At altitude, it was pretty high and even under canopy I was drifting backwards over the ground. I was thinking, "Oh shit, here we go again", but the drop zone was one of the largest on the Fort Bragg reservation. I had been released over the leading edge, so all I had to do was stay centered along the middle of the drop zone, and eventually, I would land in it but at the distant end. No big deal really, just a longer walk to the parachute turn-in point.

Well, that's exactly what happened and as I touched down, I let out the biggest war cry I could muster. I jumped up and down and made a complete fool of myself, as I celebrated the defeat of my fear. By the end of my career I had made a total of 80 military jumps and every one of them was a terrifying event.

The last leg of this journey took place a couple of months later. My doctor thought that scar tissue was pinching off the peroneal nerve, and he sent me to the Walter Reed Army Medical Center in Washington, D.C. for tests. After reviewing the results, the doctors at Walter Reed agreed to send me to a specialist. The specialist would go back into my wound and try to lift the scar tissue and create a path or tunnel area for the nerve to regenerate itself down my leg and restore the motor function to my foot. I was scheduled for the surgery in early August 1988. Two days before the planned surgery, my family and I went out on our 19-foot ski boat. My wife told me to get in the water and start skiing. She knew I could push down with my foot, so she figured I could push against the water just as a slalom skier has to. After I got up the first time, I had a great day and was exhausted by the time we got home.

I remember sitting in a lounge chair that night, watching television, when I got some of the most intense electrical currents running up and down my leg. I had gotten these feelings before, so I didn't think too much about it, until I could have sworn that I saw some movement in the big toe of my left foot.

It was such a tiny movement that I didn't believe my own eyes, so I called out to my wife and asked her to take a look. She confirmed some movement and the next morning I immediately went and showed my doctor, who performed the original surgery. He saw the same minute movement and called the specialist who was supposed to operate on me the next day. The specialist agreed over the phone that the best course of action was to let Mother Nature do her thing. They cancelled the operation right then and said, "Let's wait and see what develops." Another eight months later, my foot was at 90% recovery, which allowed me to be put back on flying status.

So, all's well that ends well. It was a long, nightmarish journey, but I survived and was able to move on with my life. My wife reminded me many years later how I kept asking her why people told me I was so lucky when they came to visit me in the hospital right after the accident. At the time I felt like the unluckiest son-of-a-bitch that had ever lived. Only after many years did I realize how truly fortunate I was. I always tell people that God must have had more work for me to do.

I would like to thank all those who had any part in allowing the Hawk to continue on. So many people were involved that it would be impossible to name them all and for fear that I might overlook someone I just want you all to know how forever grateful the Hawk truly is. Thanks again.

This was also the event and time that allowed me to understand the Raven's demons. We had both stood at the same doorway and walked away. We had both experienced an intense moment of mortality. I think back to that aircraft hanger so long ago, and the way I grilled the Raven, and why I felt embarrassed at my ignorance then and realized why he had been so reluctant to talk. I never spoke to the Raven again about the *Purple Haze* mission. I didn't need to. Now I understood.

8 THE KILLING OF LAMBCHOP

Sometimes a man has to do what a man has to do, even if it means killing Lambchop. Lambchop was the cute little hand puppet that made Shari Lewis famous. My Lambchop was completely different and I want to apologize now for its untimely death. This is how it happened.

Snuffy and Kelly Bob were two more people from the Raven's unit who were critical factors in my rehabilitation from the jump accident. About six months after my injury, Kelly Bob called and said he was putting together a jungle survival and training exercise in Guatemala in December and asked if I could help him get some aircraft to support the operation. Kelly Bob was the Operations Officer who worked for Snuffy, the Squadron Commander.

Snuffy was another legend in the Raven's unit. He was wounded in Grenada and was aware of my leg injury. I have never been sure if he sympathized with me or felt sorry for me, but he was very instrumental in the decision process allowing me to participate in this exercise. After this exercise, Snuffy gave up command of this fine unit to the Raven.

Raven's unit always wanted to train where the "shit was going down" in case we had to deploy there. It was a great training environment and allowed the operators to familiarize themselves with the area and the terrain they could fight in.

Guatemala was one of those Central American countries, like El Salvador and Nicaragua, fighting a guerilla insurgency in the mid-'80s. After many messages to the Joint Chiefs of Staff and the State Department, a team was approved to brief the ambassador and country team on a concept of operations for the exercise. I became part of the briefing team and helped coordinate the exercise. Later, I proceeded into Guatemala to take part in the exercise.

Since I was in a position to decide who would pay for these aircraft, which were quite expensive, I was in a very powerful spot. I was an air guy, and I saw some great opportunities for the aircrews to get some worthwhile training. If I could horse-trade with Kelly Bob and Snuffy, I was keen on providing the aircraft.

After the initial call from Kelly Bob, a coordination meeting was held to discuss all aspects of the operation and decide what aircraft would be required. Kelly Bob, Snuffy, Raven and the Hawk met at Raven's headquarters. Raven was the Command's Operations Officer and would coordinate final approval of the concept of operations with all outside agencies. Raven would also approve my participating in the exercise.

Kelly Bob and I decided on a C-141 Starlifter (the aircraft I was qualified in) to bring in the main body, a CASA 212 to bring in the recon team and a C-5 to carry the four Blackhawk helicopters, pilots, crew chiefs and maintenance team.

For me to authorize funds for these aircraft, I had to make sure that the aircrews would receive good training. In order to do this, I had to travel to Guatemala with Kelly Bob and check out the terrain and runways for suitability to support our intended operations. This was called a site survey and there were four other guys who accompanied us - two operations NCOs, one helicopter pilot and an operator, who would organize the jungle survival training.

The operator, who organized the survival aspect of the exercise, was one of the original soldiers selected when the unit was created ten years previously. Going through a special selection course to become part of the Raven's unit attracted people from all walks of life and varied backgrounds.

These individuals had many of the same character traits you would want in a Special Forces soldier: intelligence, maturity, physical strength, professionalism and an ability to operate isolated for long periods of time. Kelly Bob and I called this guy "Sgt. Ewell", after Ewell Gibbons, the famous naturalist who was a pitch man for Grape Nuts cereal. However, our Ewell was quite funny and kept us rolling in laughter by relating hilarious stories. Sgt. Ewell didn't even look like an operator. He wore thick glasses and was slightly overweight when I met him.

Ewell was a little older now and had a leg injury, which prevented him from running or doing physical training. He had put on some pounds, but this did not prevent him from going on this survey and coordinating the survival training. He was a good ol' country boy and loved the thought of putting together a test of his fellow soldiers' ability to operate isolated in the jungle. He was perfect for the job.

We landed in Guatemala City, rented cars and headed for our hotel, the Casino Royale. It was a beautiful hotel, located in the middle of a large Central American city. On the outskirts of Guatemala City was a sprawling mass of impoverished humanity living in squalid shacks, but the urban center of the city was just like any other large city. Tall buildings housed banks, law firms, and doctor's offices; nearby were many fine restaurants, and all the major hotel chains, like Marriot and Holiday Inn. Although civil war was ongoing in Guatemala at the time, there was no fighting in the city. Rather, it was mostly in the countryside, where the poor and desperate peasants were struggling for a better way of life. In these countries you are either very poor or very rich. There is no middle class, like the majority of Americans are.

We settled in at the hotel for the night, and the next day headed for the embassy to present our briefing to the ambassador. The presentation went flawlessly, and the ambassador gave us the green light to continue planning the exercise.

The Defense military attaché was an Army Colonel, and he assigned a Marine, working as an assistant attaché in the embassy, to help us with any support we would need from the host country. The next day, we took a commercial flight up north and landed at Santa Elena, a joint civil-military airport in the heart of the Guatemalan jungle.

This was no ordinary airport or landing strip. Carved out of the jungle were an enormous 12,000-foot asphalt runway and a huge, concrete parking ramp. The Guatemalan Air Force in 1988 consisted of eight World War II vintage P-51 Mustangs, a few A-37 Dragonflys and some Huey helicopters. The parking ramp dwarfed the number of aircraft that were parked there. I was wondering how such an impoverished country had the funds and wherewithal to build such an extremely large complex in the middle of fucking nowhere.

The Marine gave us the explanation. The good old US of A had built this airfield as a divert base for our B-52s. The Berlin Wall had not yet fallen, and we were still living in a Cold war environment and mentality.

Back in the '50s and '60s, the government decided to build bases like these throughout the world to recover our nuclear bombers in the event their bases had been attacked and destroyed by incoming Soviet nukes. The planes would have a place to land and rearm to fight another day. So, a crew could have taken off from Minot AFB, North Dakota, flown to the USSR, dropped its bombs and while flying back to the runway at Minot, been notified that Minot had been destroyed. Their aircraft, with aerial refueling, could continue on to an airfield like the one we were now standing on which would be their divert base. What an amazing facility!

I saw no problem with one of my C-141s landing blacked out here, if I could coordinate it. The Marine took us to the airfield manager, and I explained what I wanted. I needed to turn off all the runway, taxiway and hangar lights that could interfere with the pilot's landing on NVGs. He said "No problemo."

I explained I would have a combat controller place some infrared beacons alongside the runway, and have a radio to communicate and give the aircraft permission to land. All I asked for was a Crash, Fire and Rescue (CFR) truck, with crew standing by, in case of an emergency. Again he said "No problemo" and the first part of my mission was complete.

We then went to our hotel in the town of Santa Elena. This was a hotel that catered to tourists, being very clean with nice rooms. The tourism industry was the big attraction, because just due east of the town lay the ancient Mayan city of Tikal. The Tikal ruins are some of the most famous Mayan structures and rise majestically out of the middle of the jungle. They are a major tourist attraction for people around the world.

The Mayan civilization mysteriously disappeared off the face of the Earth with no explanation, but the ruins they left are incredibly beautiful reminders of what people could build even hundreds of years ago. Meticulously constructed from massive pieces of stone, Tikal, with its huge temples, is a tremendous site to see.

That night we ventured into the city for dinner. We found a nice outdoor restaurant and sat down. All of a sudden, a fleet of vehicles came to a screeching halt in front of the restaurant. A number of men, armed with submachine guns, hopped out of the cars and strategically surrounded our building. We looked at one another and wondered "What the fuck, over?"

After a few minutes, the armed men seemed satisfied that the area was secure, and a distinguished-looking officer in uniform disembarked from the back of one of the vehicles. He came directly to our table and introduced himself as Brigadier General Santos, the commander of all forces in Santa Elena. Santa Elena airfield was the major staging base for the Guatemalan military to conduct raids against the guerrillas who operated with impunity across the border into Guatemala from bases in Mexico to the northwest.

It was the General's responsibility to know this area and any unusual happenings. When seven American military-looking gringos arrived in this small place and decided to go out on the town, the word went out fairly quickly. We stuck out like sore thumbs in this poor impoverished town.

We were probably being watched as soon as we left our hotel rooms. The General wanted to know who we were and our reason for being in Santa Elena. He was an educated man and spoke fluent English.

Kelly Bob was smooth and explained how we were here to train with Guatemalan forces at the Kaibil Ranger camp about 65 kilometers to the east. The Guatemalan military had an elite unit named the Kaibil Rangers. This unit was modeled after the American Army Rangers, even down to the insignia they wore, a black t-shirt with

Kaibil in yellow letters and a yellow border curved in the same motif as the Army Ranger emblem.

The General looked us over and flashed a big, shit-eating grin. I guess he believed our explanation, because he ordered a big bottle of rum, and we commenced to drink many Cuba Libres (rum-and-cokes with a lime twist) until we were all shit-faced.

This General had been wounded seven times in combat and survived numerous assassination attempts. That was the reason for all the security when he arrived. After he got into his car and departed, we staggered back to our hotel, not realizing the potential danger we may have been in, if the bad guys had wanted to make another attempt on General Big Shot. We were trying to win the hearts and minds of the locals, so we thought it was cool to drink with the man. The next day he provided us a helicopter, and we flew to the Kaibil Ranger camp.

From the air we came upon a dirt strip cut out of the jungle and the camp itself. The camp consisted of a few wooden barracks, a mess hall, and a headquarters building, and was pretty primitive-looking. Two young Kaibil Lieutenants were assigned to us and gave us a tour of the compound. They could speak some English, and Kelly Bob could speak some Portuguese, which was close enough to Spanish, so we were at least able to communicate somewhat.

The Lieutenants first brought us to a booby trap course. The course was the most diabolical I had ever seen. The booby traps were some of the ones that the Kaibil had encountered over the years during the fighting with the guerrilla insurgency. There were all kinds of spring-loaded traps with arrows and wooden stakes that could impale a man at the slightest pressure. There was a huge log that could fall and easily crush a man's skull when a hidden wire was tripped. This was a confidence course for the Kaibil Rangers to go through.

There was also an underground maze that was so dark and forbidding that I was actually a little worried I would get lost and never find my way out. Our guides easily got us through it, and we then marched up the side of the mountain that the camp was built on.

At the top were some open training areas, well-hidden beneath the jungle canopy. Wooden benches were set up to hold classes on jungle survival and tactics training. We looked down the other side of the mountain and could see a huge lake. Ewell whispered to Kelly Bob that this would be a great jungle survival training area, and he could very easily set up the course. Kelly Bob agreed, and the first part of our site survey was completed.

Next, we needed to find a drop zone and proceeded to find one in an area south of the camp that was generally flat and covered only with a few small trees and scrub brushes. It was mostly open area and could easily accommodate 65 HALO jumpers. It was more than suitable for our purpose.

The final places to coordinate were the infiltration and exfiltration locations for the helicopters. The helos had to position the men for both the jungle survival training and for the follow-on tactical movement through the jungle. The tactical movement culminated with a raid on a small village, where some role-players were being held hostage.

After we found all the sites and marked them on our maps, we headed back to the camp. By this time, we had become good buddies with our guides and had built some rapport.

Upon our return to the camp mess hall, it was time to build some more rapport, so out came the traditional bottles of rum. We sat down and began some serious discussions recounting the day's events over many "shooters". By the end of our "discussions", we were very well shit-faced again. As we poured ourselves back into the helo for the flight back to Santa Elena, there were smiles all around, and we were confident in the knowledge that this would be a great exercise.

We returned to the States, and a few weeks later, Kelly Bob called and asked me to come down to Wally World and listen to his brief to Snuffy and the rest of the men of the unit.

This would be the squadron's first exposure to the upcoming exercise and what the men would be faced with. I will remember this day for the rest of my life. I walked in and sat at the head table with Lt. Col. Snuffy, the Squadron Commander. The men were seated all throughout the briefing room in various military uniforms and physical training gear.

The lights dimmed and a slide of a dark green jungle came into focus on the screen in front of us. At the same time, blaring from loudspeakers in the room was a song by Guns 'n' Roses titled *Welcome to the Jungle*.

I could not believe it. I looked over at Snuffy, but he didn't give any kind of signal. He just kept his stony-demeanored face looking straight forward.

What an attention-grabber I thought to myself. Here I was, sitting at the head table, in this one-of-a-kind, world-class facility, with 50 of the nation's finest professional soldiers, and we're listening to full-blast, heavy metal, rock-and-roll music and watching a slide show. Too cool!

The slides continued to show the camp, the booby-trap course, the lake, the Tikal ruins (which we flew right over on the way to the camp and were able to take pictures of) and the drop zone.

As the song finished and the slide show ended, the lights came up and Kelly Bob stood up and began his brief. He explained the objectives of the exercise and the desired learning outcomes. He then introduced Ewell, who explained the objectives of the survival training. Ewell briefed the troops on the climate, what edible plants were indigenous to the area, what was poisonous and some of the more pertinent information, such as how to build shelters and fish traps. I listened with fascination.

After the briefings were completed, Snuffy turned to me and invited me to go along on the exercise. I thought what a tremendous honor to be asked to go with them. I had been coordinating air support for this unit for three and a half years, and now I was going to be part of their world.

In early December, I pre-positioned with a Combat Controller to Santa Elena airfield. Initially, we monitored the jump over our SATCOM radio and were relieved to find out that all 65 jumpers had made it safely onto the drop zone without any injuries.

Snuffy and his men gathered up their parachutes and weapons, moved to the camp and hunkered down for the night. We then set up the beacons, shut down the lights of the airfield and waited for the giant C-141 to arrive. The C-141 had made the airdrop at last light from 10,000 feet and then descended to fly a 1000-foot low-level blacked-out route to the airfield for training.

As the airplane made its final approach, all the Guatemalan pilots and airfield personnel came out to watch this monster-sized aircraft land with no lights. I can only imagine what their thoughts were as this was unfolding. Crazy Americans! The aircraft made a perfect landing and taxied into parking, still with no lights on. The night was completely black with no moon visible. After the aircraft was parked, the clamshell doors opened in the rear, and we offloaded the rest of Snuffy's and his men's equipment for the next two weeks of training.

I visited with the aircrew and thanked them for their superb performance. I knew the pilot from when I was stationed at Charleston AFB four years earlier. He thanked me for making the training available to his crew and to get out of the local pattern and do something completely different. The crew had flown nonstop from Fort Bragg to the airdrop over a Guatemalan jungle and then flown a low-level route to a first-time, blacked-out landing at a base never before attempted.

After the offload was completed, they taxied out to

the runway, took off and returned to Charleston AFB in South Carolina. It was all in a day's work.

It was wonderful to be able to work back in the early days of the command. It seemed like whatever we young Turks could come up with for training was allowed as long as we did our homework, planned accordingly and operated safely.

Later that evening, the four Blackhawks arrived at Santa Elena from Honduras. Honduras could better support the C-5 that hauled them from the States. Santa Elena could have done just as well, but did not have the equipment to offload and build up the helicopters. Tegucigalpa Air Base in Honduras could manage both, so that's where they went.

After the flight from Honduras, the crews went to the hotel in Santa Elena for a last night on the town before flying to the Kaibil camp the next morning.

There was some sort of feast going on that night and most of the locals were at a big festival downtown. The Guatemalan Air Force pilots came to the hotel and invited the Army chopper pilots and me to join them.

We then proceeded to do what all pilots do all over the world. We grabbed a table in the center of the festival, ordered drinks all around, proceeded to get shit-faced, and ogled all the pretty girls as they walked by. We made numerous rude comments, swapped war stories and generally made fools of ourselves. Typical "pilot bullshit" but it was so much fun, and we built instant friendships.

The Guatemalans were interchangeable for so many others. The Raven and I had made so many friends around the world; Brits, Thais, Jordanians, Israelis and the list went on. I regret never having the opportunity to go back and renew most of those friendships. That was just the nature of our business. Get in, get out and move on - whether it be a real-world operation or a social situation.

Early next morning, I boarded one of the Black-hawks with all the equipment from the C-141 that had been transloaded to the helos for transport to the camp. As the sun came up, the four helos fired up their engines. Blades swirling, they roared into the humid air. We then proceeded to thunder across the jungle at treetop level heading for the camp.

It was tremendously heady stuff. Legs dangling out the side of the helo, I was in my jungle fatigues (Vietnam-era style and very light-weight), wore a survival vest and carried an overnight bag. My boss back home approved my attending only the initial jungle survival training, and then I had to hustle back to Fort Bragg.

This front-end jungle survival training would last just three days, and then I would fly back on a commercial airliner. I couldn't justify staying and running around the jungle for two weeks and putting an undue amount of work on my office mates. They knew I had put a lot of effort into supporting this exercise with the command's money, so they gave me some slack.

After a twenty-minute flight, we landed on the dirt strip, which was actually quite muddy. That was the only part of the exercise that didn't happen as Kelly Bob and I had planned. The rainy season (unknown and unplanned for) was in full force in Central America.

The rain came down like a water faucet turned full open at times. The dirt strip was too muddy and rutted to safely land the CASA 212 aircraft. We had to cancel that portion of the exercise. The recon team had to come on a commercial flight as part of the advance force with the medical personnel (provided for safety purposes) who would support the drop zone for Snuffy and his troops.

As I jumped off the helo, Kelly Bob grabbed me and showed me where to throw my gear, except for my survival vest, and then led me to an outdoor briefing area located in front of the Kaibil Ranger headquarters building. Snuffy and his men were already seated and I grabbed a seat alongside him and Kelly Bob.

We must have taught the Kaibil Rangers well when they attended our American schools for Airborne, Ranger and Special Forces qualifications. They had their own attention grabber. From behind us, two Kaibil Rangers came running, carrying a huge boa constrictor. It must have been at least ten feet long with an enormous body. They threw this snake at our feet and taunted it with sticks so that it would try to attack them. I was sitting in stunned amazement. I was sure the other 65 guys were thinking the same thing. "What have we gotten ourselves into?"

The camp commander then came out, introduced himself in somewhat broken English and welcomed us to Guatemala and the Kaibil Ranger camp.

There was somewhat of a hidden agenda, I suppose, behind all this. The Guatemalans may have believed that good old Uncle Sugar (as we referred to Uncle Sam at times) would provide their military with the latest weapons, ammunition and technology to help fight the insurgency in return for allowing us to train in their country. The Guatemalans pulled out all the stops in supporting this training. I don't know if the Guatemalan government ever actually received anything for this training, because that decision was made way above my pay grade.

After the short introduction, our hosts asked us to follow them, and we began to hump up the mountain toward the training area. It was only a kilometer and a half, but it was straight up and great therapy for my Turkey leg. By the time we got to the top, we were all drenched in sweat from the heat and humidity. We grabbed seats on some wooden benches and the lectures began.

One of the Snuffy's men spoke fluent Spanish and translated for us. The Kaibil Rangers brought out four animals: a chicken, a jungle rat, a very large sea turtle and a sheep. The latter was Lambchop and Lambchop was now doomed.

They explained that these are the kinds of animals we could encounter in the jungle during our survival training, and if we could catch one, we could kill and eat it. They would demonstrate how to kill them.

When asked by the Kaibil demonstrator how we wanted to see the chicken killed, he offered two options. He could twist the head off with his bare hands, or he could bite the head off with his teeth.

Now, what option do you think the bloodthirsty Americans opted for? Snuffy's men were all shouting for the soldier to bite the head off the chicken. I watched in gruesome fascination as the Kaibil Ranger did just that. With a smile he calmly bit off the head of the chicken. When he completed severing the head with his teeth, we all clapped and the soldier smiled with chicken blood dripping from his mouth. It was not a pretty picture.

The jungle rat looked just like what it was. It was the largest, ugliest looking rat I had ever seen. It was tied upside down by all four legs, hanging from a bamboo shoot. They easily chopped off its head with a machete and moved on to the turtle. The turtle was flipped onto its back and held in place by a couple of soldiers. A third soldier grabbed the machete and whacked the soft under-side of the turtle's belly, splitting it in two. They showed us how to get the meat out and make turtle soup. Again, I was fascinated by what was going on, but what happened next is still a little hard for me to believe sometimes.

The sheep was strung upside down and hung from some wooden poles. The demonstrator started jabbering in Spanish to our translator and gesturing at the crowd. Snuffy's man said something in return and the next thing I knew, this guy was headed for me!

He handed me a razor-sharp knife, grabbed my arm and dragged me toward the sheep. He and another soldier then grabbed the head of the sheep and pulled it down and backwards over a pail. He then gave me this slashing signal with his hand across his throat. He wanted me to cut the throat of poor Lambchop! I had never butchered a live animal before that I could remember. I think I had maybe cut up a frog in ninth-grade biology, but this was completely different!

The Hawk was not mentally prepared to kill Lamb-chop, but the war chants began from the crowd. "Do it! Kill it!" came the cries of the cutthroat, blood- thirsty warriors sitting behind me. What could I do? I leaned down and gingerly put the knife against the throat of the sheep and gently pulled it back and forth in a little saw-ing motion.

The Kaibil Ranger then screamed at me "Mas! Mas!" ("More! More!"), and I proceeded to make a harder at-tempt with the slashing motion of my knife. The next thing I knew there was fucking blood everywhere! The sheep's blood was all over my hands, my uniform, and the knife I held. I stood there horrified for a few seconds and watched the bright red blood pour out of the throat of this poor animal into the pail below it. Someone took some pictures of this event as I backed away, and I was later seen to be as pale as a ghost.

The American and the Guatemalan soldiers took great pleasure at my discomfort and in the pictures they were laughing and clapping hysterically. I sat back down next to Snuffy and all he said was, "Ya done good."

I found out later that when the men came out of the survival phase, the animals we had just killed had been prepared for a special feast, to celebrate the conclusion of that phase of training. I did complete the jungle sur-vival phase, but would miss the feast and the devouring of poor Lambchop.

After a few more briefings about the dangers of the jungle, we hiked to a landing zone and were immediately airlifted out by the helos and flown to an open area by the lake. Sgt. Ewell was there and formed the men up, then marched them into the jungle. He placed a man every 400 meters or so and told each soldier to avoid contact with others until he returned to pick up each individual soldier in two days time.

They would be graded on the shelter they built, a fish trap built in the lake waters and an animal trap. For grading criteria, the more elaborately the shelter and the traps were constructed, the higher the grade. A prize would be given to the winner. The prize turned out to be a Guatemalan machete.

After placing all the men in the jungle, Sgt. Ewell took me, a radio operator, a doctor and two Operations NCOs, known as Carlos the Pirate and the Wildman, to a location farther down the trail. It was near the water, and we set up a base camp. If any soldier got in trouble, each one had a radio and could make contact with the base camp, and we would respond in a hurry.

I asked what my job was, and they said to not get hurt or lost. What a way to spend jungle survival training I thought, but I wasn't about to complain!

I opened one of the pouches on my aviator's survival vest and found a hook and some thread. I headed off to the lake to try my luck at fishing. I loved to fish and took pride in the fact that I usually caught something, but I didn't catch a damned thing in that lake. I don't know if there really were fish in that lake because I didn't see any.

When the exercise was over, Ewell found one soldier who had feasted on a large trout he had caught. I don't know how he did it, but 65 other guys didn't catch shit!

After my futile fishing adventure, I returned to the base camp as the sun was going down. I was hungry, but we had nothing to eat.

We built a fire for the night and commenced to tell amusing stories. Carlos the Pirate kept us in stitches with his imitations of a blustery pirate lost in the jungle, until we all fell asleep for the night.

The next morning our radio operator, Danny, who was of Spanish descent, noticed a thatched hut just down the lake from us with some smoke drifting from it. He ventured out and came back with four eggs. He had exchanged some dollars for Guatemalan money before he left the States and made an offer the lady of the house could not refuse. I don't know how much he paid, but those eggs split among the six of us were a great treat. He called it winning the hearts and minds of the locals. I was learning an important lesson.

Carlos went on a food-finding mission of his own. He was a fairly big man and had a machete. He found a palm heart tree and chopped it down. He came and got us, and we carried it back to the base camp. The rest of the day we spent cutting up the tree and eating the inside, which was actually the palm heart. I don't know if I would recommend this as a meal, but it sure tasted good when you're hungry.

I then made probably the most foolish remark of my life. I said, "This jungle survival training is way too easy." This was about six o'clock in the evening and Sgt. Ewell told me to grab my survival vest and follow him. We walked far into the jungle and came to a stop, as it was getting fairly dark. Ewell handed me a 9mm Beretta with two clips of bullets, a flash- bang grenade and a radio. He said if I got into trouble to throw the grenade to mark my position and make a radio call as quickly as possible. Who knows what could be out here? Bad guys and bad animals!

"Great, just fucking great," I was thinking to myself. Ewell also said I could use whatever I had in my survival vest, as I was role-playing a simulated downed airman. He then told me he would come back for me the next morning. I said, "You've got to be kidding!" as he turned his back and disappeared into the jungle from the way we came. He looked over his shoulder and casually said "I'll see you tomorrow."

I didn't think this survival training would be too difficult, but it turned out to be the worst fifteen hours of my life. I opened another pouch on my vest and pulled out what is called a space blanket. If the soldiers knew I had this, they would have probably killed me for it. It was a silvery-looking sheet that I could wrap myself in. Ewell had put me out so late that I did not have enough time to build a shelter. I did find a huge palm frond growing out of the jungle floor and laid my space blanket down under it and tried to get some sleep. Boy was I fucking wrong!

First, the jungle really comes alive at night. The sounds become magnified and my imagination was running rampant, thinking some wild animal was about to find me and make me its next meal. I clutched the 9mm Beretta in one hand and the grenade in the other. Then the fucking rain started! The rain dripped off the palm frond and began to pool in my space blanket.

With the rain falling harder and harder, the temperature dropped quickly and I became one cold, miserable son-of-a-bitch.

I remember plotting out the rest of my life during the night. I couldn't wait for daylight. I had some fire cubes in my vest and I figured I could start a fire at first light and dry myself out.

After what seemed like an eternity and no sleep at all, it slowly started to get light out and the rain stopped. By now, every part of me was thoroughly soaked. The rain was gone but replaced with a dense mist. It was so misty that I couldn't see but maybe 10 to 15 feet. The mist hung in the air like a spider's web. I holstered my weapon, laid the grenade down next to the radio and started to gather some twigs.

Everything was solidly wet through and through, but I was determined. I made a little tepee-like structure, put a fire cube under it, and lit it with a match from a book that was also in the survival vest. The fire cube was not hot enough to dry out the twigs, and all I was getting were some twigs that became glowing embers.

I knelt down and did my best imitation of the Big Bad Wolf and commenced to huff and puff on this pitiful attempt at a fire. I blew 'til I was red in the face, when I suddenly got a small puff of smoke and a tiny flame. I thought I was in ecstasy as my fire was starting, but it quickly died out, and the smoke drifted into the jungle.

I wasn't about to give up. I got another cube out and started the whole process over again. It was getting lighter out, but the mist still hung like cotton candy throughout the jungle.

I was leaning down, concentrating on blowing on the embers to help ignite the fire, when I got the scare of my life. I heard a voice from behind me say "Hello." I looked behind me and an apparition like a ghost appeared out of the fog. I saw Indian Jack staring at me from no more than ten feet away. His face was totally camouflaged with black paint, he had a mosquito net draped over the jungle boonie hat he was wearing, and he had a CAR-15 assault rifle cradled in his arms. He just smiled at me with the whitest teeth I had ever seen and said, "I smelled your smoke." I was too stunned to answer. He quickly turned and disappeared back into the jungle mist. I had never heard him approach my position.

My immediate thought was if this guy could sneak up on me so silently, then I could have been a dead man very easily. After he left me alone again, I remembered a feeling of great comfort came over me knowing that he was on my side, and it should be of great pride to this nation that we have good men like him in our military.

Later, I found out Indian Jack was from some- place in New Mexico and he, too, had Indian blood in him. He was also the interpreter that set me up with the earlier sheep operation. This smoke episode later became very important to me and I could easily relate to it, when the Raven told me about throwing his cigarettes away before he went on his infamous recon mission in Vietnam.

Finally, the sun broke through the thick mist, and Sgt. Ewell came and got me just as I was starting to dry out. We returned to the base camp and I told my war story about Indian Jack sneaking up on me to Carlos, Wildman and Danny as Ewell continued to collect everybody from along the lake.

When everybody was back at the base camp, the helicopters were called in to extract us to the Kaibil camp. Our reward when we got back was a Meal Ready to Eat (MRE). I had a ham slice with cheese and crackers. After only two-thirds of an egg and some palm heart over three days, I was starving. It was the best MRE I have ever eaten.

After a quick shower, I grabbed my gear and hopped a helo back to Santa Elena. My commercial flight brought me back to Guatemala City and the next morning I was on my way back to Fort Bragg. It was a tremendously gratifying experience. As an Air Force C-141 pilot, I was allowed to enter a very special world and experience what others can only dream of. My thanks to Snuffy, Kelly Bob and the Raven for allowing it to happen.

9 THIRD TIME'S A CHARM

The hunt for General Manuel Noriega lasted for two years, and his luck was about to run out. On our third deployment together, the Raven and the Hawk were victorious and helped bring him to justice.

In 1987, I moved to a new job at our Command's headquarters and was responsible for creating the command-and-control document that would be a sort of written plan for the Panamanian invasion.

When Manny (as we jokingly referred to him) began operating beyond the scope of a benevolent dictator, it was time for us to take action. Orders came down for us to begin planning an operation against Manuel Noriega and the forces that were keeping him in power.

His henchmen were called the Panamanian Defense Force or PDF for short. Their headquarters, known as La Commandancia, was about 30 kilometers to the east of Howard Air Force Base and across the Bridge of the

Americas. A quick reaction force of specially-trained thugs was known as Battalion 2000, and they were located at Rio Hato airfield to the north of Panama City.

In May 1989, Noriega overturned a democratically elected government and had the newly-elected Vice President Billy Ford beaten in a bloody confrontation. The picture of the Vice President, with his head covered in blood, was splashed on the front page of newspapers and magazines all over the world. It became a vivid reminder of the oppressive regime Manny and the PDF had become.

A squadron of the Raven's men and a small battle staff, to include me and two ex-operators turned "staff pukes" called Critter and Squid, were rapidly deployed in the middle of the night.

We landed on the runway at Howard; taxied in and parked, deplaned, and walked into a place we soon called "Hangar Three, the Movie." We called it that because we did everything there. We slept, shaved, planned, played poker, swapped war stories and generally lived in there for a month. A guy we named Nobi (named after Nobi Beri - the leader of the Amal faction in Beirut) was writing a diary which he wanted to convert into a screenplay to help pass the time away.

Nobi fancied himself as the action star, Chuck Norris, and he was the star of this movie, but he actually looked more like the nerdy television character Steve Urkel. He also had Jabba the Hutt (from *Star Wars*) starring as Manuel Noriega and the baldheaded Yul Brynner playing the role of Doc.

As each day passed, Nobi continued to make entries, and this was how Nobi briefly described our arrival and new life in the hangar. "The look on his face was one of utter pain…as the wheels of the massive C-141 engraved their black marks on the runway at Howard Air Force Base, Nobi could tell that this time, like all the others, he would get sick…violently sick." Nobi hated puking but "John Wayne" Steve hated it even more, since he was the one Nobi was puking on.

As the aircrew waited for the Customs officials to near the plane before opening the cargo door, Nobi thrust his second heave into the air. With the force of a volcanic eruption, Nobi hit the foreign Customs officials with the remains of a partially digested ham and banana sandwich on rye.

When they arrived at the hangar most of the passengers did not even bother to set up their cots. The flight had been long and the turbulence made the guys as nervous as a whore in church. Only "Mittens" enjoyed the flight, but then, Mittens enjoyed shit like that anyway.

"These badges will get you anything in this country you guys want," explained the King of Secret Squirrel and the inventor of the secret handshake, Mr. Ed. "This badge will not only get you into the pool here, but it will also get you a free, six-piece box of Panamanian chicken". "Arghhh" Nobi moaned as traces of ham chunks lingered within his interproximal incisors. "Chicken sounds good to me," mentioned the Rabbit. The Rabbit was an intellectual man in his mid-twenties, but the wars in Central America had not been kind to him. Rabbit was thin and looked more like a man in his seventies.

Nobi's last entry in his screenplay described the weather. He explained, "A man known as Lightning was the weather guesser, along with his youngest son, Darth Vader. They studied charts of the area in hopes of just once predicting the weather correctly. The weather was hot and the humidity high with the usual rain in the late afternoon. It had been this way since the beginning of time, but yet Laurel and Hardy (Lightning and Darth Vader) had a difficult time making their predictions." Nonsensical at times, but for those of us who lived there, we understood it all.

This deployment lasted about a month, then we were recalled to the States in June, as the situation in Panama somewhat stabilized when Noriega resumed power.

In October of the same year, a small cadre of Noriega's men attempted a coup. Noriega called for the thugs of Battalion 2000, who flew in from Rio Hato and immediately crushed the small uprising. As this was going on, the Critter, Nobi, Raven and his men, and I deployed again to Hangar Three. Nobi renamed his screenplay "Hangar Three, the Never-Ending Story-Part II: Bullets for Noriega or How I Learned to Live and Love a Hangar." This is when we began some serious training evolutions for operations that would be conducted if the politicians gave us the green light to execute a Panamanian "rescue mission."

An American, Kurt Muse, was being held in the notorious Modelo prison. A four-story building, it was located across the street from La Commandancia, Noriega's headquarters. Through our intelligence sources we learned much about Modelo. We knew the exact location of the prison cell where Muse was being held. We knew how many guards there were, their locations in watch-towers and within the prison itself, and their shift hours. We knew the PDF was expecting a potential assault at the ground floor and had reinforced their positions with sandbags and a machine gun nest. They never expected an assault from the roof.

On the base at Howard, the closest replica to the prison was a building where the children of military personnel attended elementary school. (An interesting fact I found out later was that Raven's boss, the Coyote, had attended this same school when he was twelve years old.) We rehearsed on top of this school building.

The Raven and his men planned a rescue operation which required four MH-6 "slicks" loaded with personnel to land on top of the building. A plywood structure was built to simulate the entrance the men would have to breach to get down into the prison where the American was being held. He was in a cell two stories down from the top of the roof. We conducted the rehearsal at night, simulating the conditions we would encounter during the actual execution of the real mission.

We had a few misadventures as we executed the rehearsal. There was a three-foot high wall around the top of the building and one of the little birds accidentally struck it with its tail boom as he was landing. Fortunately no one was hurt and the aircraft was repaired and flown back before daylight. Imagine the kids coming to school the next day and seeing this flat black-painted, little helicopter sitting on top of their school! What questions would they have asked and what about the teachers? They could possibly have tipped off the PDF that the Americans were up to something.

Another Murphy hit us during the exfil phase. We used the bigger and more powerful UH-60 Blackhawk to land on the roof, pick up the assault force and the rescued hostage, and bring them back to the airfield. Despite our good intentions of building that wooden structure and placing it in the exact location as the one on top of Modelo, we had not anchored it in place. As the larger helicopter began its approach onto the roof, the aircraft's tremendous rotor wash effectively lifted the wooden structure into the air. The structure easily broke apart with large pieces of plywood flying everywhere and becoming airborne missiles. Again, we were very lucky and nobody was hit by the falling debris. Most of the stuff fell harmlessly to the ground and we were able to police it up before daylight. We would do better next time and secure the structure in place.

Another night we planned and executed a live fire rehearsal. This was really awesome.

At sunset, our Deputy Commanding General, a radio-transmitter operator (RTO), a Combat Controller, and I, plus a few others who were to compose the Assault CP, were combat floor-loaded into a Blackhawk at Howard airfield. We camouflaged our faces, which were smeared in black, green and brown tones. We carried weapons and fully-loaded clips of ammunition.

Four more Blackhawks carried the Raven, his men, and a medical support team. We flew to an open field half way up the Panama Canal called Gatun for final planning and coordination. After reviewing the plan with the General, Raven's men then transloaded to four smaller MH-6's for their mission and the assault CP reboarded their Blackhawk. The medical support guys remained at Gatun with a medevac helicopter assigned to them.

We lifted off first and headed for a location called Battery MacKenzie. Raven and his men headed for Battery Pratt. These sites were abandoned bunkers situated at the north end of the Panama Canal, and once contained several very large cannons used to defend against invaders. The location was very remote and ideal for our rehearsal. We could fire live rounds and breach with real explosives.

Our helicopter was much faster than theirs, and we arrived at our location much sooner than Raven's assault team. We quickly jumped off the helo; set up our radios and sat back and listened to the "op" go down. Our helo then flew back to Gatun to wait for us to call for pick up after the rehearsal was completed. Battery Mackenzie and Battery Pratt were only a couple of kilometers apart and we monitored the execution checklist. If things "went to shit", we could immediately call in the medical helo with the doctors and PJs from Gatun.

Leading the formation were two "Killer Eggs" (AH-6s). Their mission was to fire rockets and miniguns into two wooden structures which we had built at Battery Pratt to simulate the watch towers at Modelo prison. As

I listened and watched from my position a short distance away, the night sky was lit up by the rocket explosions and the minigun's red tracers. These structures were quickly destroyed, eliminating the immediate threat and making the arrival less hazardous for the assault helos.

As the AH-6s completed their gun run and peeled off, the assault helos quickly followed and offloaded the assaulters. The Raven's men breached another wooden structure specially built on top of the bunker and fired live rounds into a number of target silhouettes. A role player simulating the American being held at Modelo was rescued and brought out of the bunker.

Raven called in his exfiltration helos and the assault CP called for theirs. We all loaded up, rejoined in the air with all five Blackhawks in formation, and headed for Howard at the other end of the canal.

I vividly remember dangling my legs out the side of the helo as we cruised low-level down the Panama Canal at 180 knots, completely blacked-out, thinking, "If Noriega only knew." We were in his "backyard" and rehearsing for a potential real live mission. Talk about a rush! I was a long way from my days as a C-141 pilot, but the feelings I experienced when momentous things happened in my life were always resurrected somehow, and this was one of those moments.

On this second deployment, some days were very slow, as we had to search for training locations and build targets. We then had to plan and brief the rehearsal mission before we could execute it. These days all seemed to run together. We would walk to the chow hall for our three meals to break up the day and get out of the hangar. In the brutally hot and humid afternoon, I would go with the Critter for our daily three-mile run out to the horse stables. Afterwards, we would hit the gym and lift weights for an hour and finish up with a shower.

A few years later, there was a popular movie starring Bill Murray, the former star of the television show *Saturday Night Live*, whose character kept waking up and realizing it was the same day every day, and it happened to be on *Groundhog Day*. Well, some of our days were groundhog days. Looking back, though, these monotonously repetitive days provided us the opportunity to practice and practice until we got it right.

After another month of planning and executing rehearsal missions, the American politicians couldn't make up their minds about what to do in Panama. In early November, we redeployed to Fort Bragg.

As we were packing up and leaving, I wondered if we were ever going to execute this mission. We would get our hopes up so high, only to have them dashed. A lingering distaste for the mission began to set in. However, in early December, we were directed to conduct a full-scale rehearsal of the Panama rescue mission.

Three Ranger Battalions parachuted onto Duke Field and Tyndall AFB runways in Florida, simulating Rio Hato and Torrijos Tocumen airfields in Panama. Their mission would be to engage Battalion 2000 and prevent any reinforcements to the PDF in Panama City. It was determined that controlling the airfields was paramount to the success of the plan.

When I moved to my new job at the Command's headquarters, I made sure the guy who replaced me would be a good dude, but he turned out to be much better than me. The Scorpion was the guy I had groomed and hired to replace me in my old unit.

The Scorpion was my alter ego. He was a brilliant thinker, while I considered myself an operator - the guy who could execute a mission after it was created by the thinker. The Scorpion would plan to the finest detail and cover all the bases. I would sometimes shoot from the hip.

We were both warriors in our own respective ways, but he was more cerebral. I was the blue-collar, get-the-job-done guy. The Scorpion was in charge of developing the air plan supporting the three Ranger battalions and their airborne assault onto the two airfields.

The mission that the Raven and the Hawk had been involved in from the start was the Modelo prison rescue operation. This rehearsal was so realistic and detailed that an exact replica of the Modelo prison was built. At a taxpayer cost of $200,000 dollars in lumber, a wooden structure was built to the exact dimensions as the prison in Panama. That's the way we did things. We tried to spend the American taxpayers' money wisely, but who can determine the actual price for the life of an American citizen held in a hostage situation?

A quote from the Raven came to mind as we discussed this situation. Many people on the conventional side of the military were always complaining about how much money was being spent on training and equipping Raven and his men. His outlook was pretty straightforward and to the point. He said, "If you want the Dallas Cowboys, you have to pay for the Dallas Cowboys!" (The Cowboys have been Super Bowl Champions more than any other pro team). My sentiments exactly, and I used that quote every time I fought for equipment and personnel.

As the Florida rehearsal mission unfolded and our brave warriors landed on the rooftop of the wooden building replicating Modelo, the soldiers were able to look through the plywood cupola structure down to the cell where the role-playing hostage was being held. Peering through the cracks in the plywood, the men realized that blowing the door with an explosive charge might hurt anyone directly below. Instead, they used bolt cutters to cut the lock and made their way down to the holding cell. Other than the different entry method, the entire rehearsal went exactly according to plan.

At the rehearsal debrief, the four-star General, responsible for all Special Ops personnel and equipment, was concerned that the rehearsal did not happen exactly as planned. "The men were supposed to use explosives to breach the door, not bolt cutters," he remarked.

The Raven and his special operators briefed the potential seriousness of the situation to the General. They explained how the role-playing hostage in the holding cell was extremely exposed and, how the explosive charge used to breach the door on the rooftop would probably send dangerous debris down onto him. The flying debris might cause a serious injury. The Raven's men made the decision right then to forgo the explosive charge and use the bolt cutter to cut the lock.

After the debriefing was completed, the General kept the cut lock on his desk as a memento to remind him to "stay out of the weeds." He now tells this story to younger Generals about how he needed to remain at the strategic level in his thought process and leave the tactical level to the on-scene commander. The rehearsal was a huge success and the "four-star" reported to the politicians in DC that his forces were ready.

On a very cold night in mid-December, Hawk's beeper suddenly went off. I called my boss at home and asked him what was going on. He said to pack my bags because "We are going to do it!" I wondered what he meant as I drove in to our headquarters. When I walked in, he said we were going to Panama tonight and that President Bush had approved our plan.

I was really caught off guard to hear these words, but I grabbed my gear and headed for the plane. Four hours later, I was in Hangar Three again with Critter, Squid, Raven, his men and about 1,000 other special operators (SEALS, combat controllers, medics, little- bird pilots and battle staff pukes, to name a few). The battle staff immediately planned missions and prepared briefings while the operators prepped their weapons and gear.

The operation known as Just Cause commenced at 0045 hours on December 20th, 1989. I had been involved in the planning of this rescue mission for two years now, and it felt somewhat anti-climatic. I was in the battle staff radio room as I monitored the launch of twelve C-141s and twenty-four C-130s loaded with Rangers. Just prior to H-Hour, I walked outside the hangar with Critter and Squid.

Critter was an ex-operator from the Raven's unit and Squid was from an equivalent Navy unit. They were really depressed knowing that their buddies were going into combat and they were stuck being battle staff officers at the Command's headquarters. Timing is everything sometimes, and this was no exception for these guys.

The actual commencement of the entire "rescue mission" was to be a 105-round special delivered by an AC-130 Spectre gunship into La Commandancia. We wanted to see and hear that round since we were only 30 kilometers away by road but 6 miles as the crow flies.

We were still in disbelief that the whole mission was actually going to happen until we looked up into the night sky and saw and heard that first round go off followed by a number of others. As close as we were, the sounds traveled right to our location at Howard.

We looked at each other in silent admiration, knowing the efforts we had put forth the last two years were now paying off right before our disbelieving eyes. We then walked back into the Joint Operations Center, took our places at the battle staff tables and listened to the war unfold on our tactical and satellite radios.

The rescue of Kurt Muse was high drama!

Raven's troop commander was known as the Fridge (because he was built like one) or, as he preferred to be called, Lobo. He was a giant of a man and always tried to crush my hand when he shook it. I always wondered why, as I was no threat to him. Later, I found out he always tried to squeeze a man's hand to excess when he shook it. It was just the way the Fridge was. As I watched the Raven and Lobo leave the hangar for their mission, I wished my friend, "Godspeed."

The two AH-6 gunships, four MH-6 slicks mounted with six operators each, including the Raven, and a command-and-control (C2) UH-60 Blackhawk aircraft, with my old friend Snuffy on board, launched from Howard AFB toward Modelo Prison. The C2 helicopter was specially modified with a drop-in communications console suite. The console would allow Snuffy to relay critical information via secure line-of-sight (LOS) communications between the assault helicopters and the Joint Operations Center back at Hangar Three. Snuffy could call for help if the Raven and his men got in trouble. A quick reaction force was held in reserve at the hangar and could quickly fly to the rescue.

At H-Hour, the two "Killer Eggs" opened fire on the watch towers as planned and destroyed them both. One of the aircraft was not so lucky and was shot down by small arms' fire. The two pilots crash-landed their helicopter into the La Commandancia compound. With 105 rounds from the AC-130 gunship landing all around them, the pilots, miraculously uninjured, unbuckled and jumped out of their wrecked machine. As they ran toward the compound wall, a PDF soldier surrendered to them! The three of them then hopped the wall and ran to safety.

The small MH-6 helos staggered their landings by twos onto the prison roof and offloaded the Raven and his men. A flagpole on the roof (potential helo obstacle) and the door to the cupola were immediately blown with C4 charges by the breachers.

Snipers took up positions at the four corners of the roof to provide security protection and warn if any threat was headed their way. A four-man team (to include my old planning partner, Slammer) made their way down the stairs to Muse's cell. The American operators threw flash-bang stun grenades into the area and sent two guards to their maker, as it was later recounted to me. Through the smoke and noise of the war going on around them, Slammer yelled at the man in the cell "Are you Muse?"

The shaken and disheveled-looking man nodded, as he looked at this wild-looking man dressed in a black ninja jumpsuit and black ski mask with big white eyes staring at him through the eyeholes. Muse heard the words "We're here to rescue you!" and thought Slammer was the best sight he had ever seen in his life.

Muse was instructed to lie on the floor. The operators quickly set a charge and blew the cell door off its hinges. Slammer grabbed Muse and with the rest of the team headed for the roof.

As they got to the roof, Slammer watched the Raven take his helmet off and throw it away disgustedly. At this critical time in the operation, the Raven's communications had failed and he was a little "pissed off." Thankfully, his Saber hand-held radio, which had a throat mike, was still working and he made the call to Snuffy for extraction.

An MH-6 landed on the rooftop and immediately loaded up Muse and five operators and flew off.

Unfortunately, the aircraft was way too heavy and

crashed into an adjoining street. Two men were subsequently shot in the leg, one suffered a concussion and went unconscious, and one smashed his foot, which would eventually cost him his toes. Remarkably, the pilots and Muse escaped unharmed. An emergency radio call was then made. They were immediately rounded up by a friendly ground force of armored vehicles commanded by "Redneck", Raven's XO, which was in the vicinity, and brought back to Hangar Three.

The Raven called again on the Saber radio to Snuffy to have the other MH-6s return to extract the remaining men. Only four men got on the next aircraft, including Lobo, and the helo immediately took off. While sitting on the pod of his aircraft, Lobo saw what he described as three blazing basketballs flash by. These were later determined to be .50 cal-rounds.

On the way back to the rooftop, Lobo's pilot, Rick, was shot through his arm by a 7.62 round. It was unknown to Lobo, until he arrived back at the launch site at Howard and enthusiastically grabbed Rick's arm to thank him for the safe flight. Knowing Lobo and the reputation he had for his powerful grip, he was a little surprised when Rick screamed. In all the excitement, he didn't realize that it was from the excruciating pain of the gunshot wound and not his powerful grip that caused the pilot to scream.

The Raven's men continued to load helos and fly off the rooftop, but the number of men riding the small helicopters back out had somehow gotten "dicked up" in the noise and confusion as the battle for La Commandancia raged around them. Raven and four other men were still on the rooftop waiting for their ride, when he decided to use a much larger Blackhawk to get the last load out.

Although his helo presented a larger target, the pilot, Bobby Grapes, didn't hesitate to get the remaining five men off the roof. He swooped in and quickly flared onto the roof, taking twenty rounds of small arms' fire (the bullet holes in the fuselage were counted when the helicopter returned to Howard). Raven and his men rapidly jumped into the back of the Blackhawk and the helicopter roared off into the night sky which was lit up like a Christmas tree by all the red tracers and explosions.

The total amount of time spent in rescuing Kurt Muse, from the arrival of the first helicopter onto the building rooftop, executing the operation and extracting him, was no more than 9 minutes! Raven spent an additional 30 minutes on top of the roof before he was able to get everybody out including himself.

I was so glad to see my friend walk back into the hangar that night. He had truly just written a piece of special operations history. The first and only known rescue of an American citizen in a combat environment was successfully accomplished and my friend, the Raven, led the operation.

Later, President Bush, in a private ceremony at the White House, would personally present Raven with the Bronze Star for Valor and the Slammer with a Silver Star for their actions at Modelo prison.

The Command still had a lot of work to do, and it was another two weeks before we were done. On December 22, Raven was flown to Rio Hato airfield. The field had been secured during the initial assault and was now controlled by American forces. Raven linked up with the 3rd Battalion, 75th Rangers to plan a rescue mission to Pinome Prison.

Pinome Prison was where the PDF leaders of the aborted October coup were being held. A company of Rangers from 3/75, about 150 soldiers, would provide the firepower and security for Raven and his men as they raided the prison in an attempt to rescue the coup leaders.

One of Raven's sons had enlisted in the Army during the previous summer, went to airborne school and reported to the 2nd Battalion, 75th Rangers at Fort Lewis, Washington. Five months later, the kid found himself parachuting onto Rio Hato airfield in the initial invasion. He was only nineteen years old!

Raven sought his son out when he got to the airfield and greeted him with a big bear-hug. A picture was taken of father and son, and they shared their respective war stories over an MRE. After this quick and quiet reunion, the Raven had to get back to business. He wished his son well and headed to the Battalion Tactical Operations Center (TOC).

After coordinating the ground scheme of maneuver and sending me a request for helicopter support, the Raven returned to Hangar Three. As the men prepared their equipment and reviewed the plan, word came in that the prison guards had been told if they did not surrender, an AC-130 gunship was prepared to fire on their position and "blow their shit to kingdom come." They could not surrender quickly enough. The mission was aborted and the Raven and his men stood down.

This down time didn't last for long though, as an intelligence source indicated Noriega was hiding out in Las Tablas, a province in Panama. Noriega had been on the run from the minute the "rescue operation" started. One of our primary objectives was to capture Manny. This is when the Eagle flights commenced.

Raven and his men would load up in four Blackhawks, and a platoon (40 men) of Rangers and their specially-modified vehicles would load onto two Chinooks. The force would look for any open area near a village and set the helos down. The Rangers would provide security at the LZ for the helos and be prepared to act as a quick reaction force for Raven's assault team. Raven and his men would then head into the villages and commence house-to-house searches.

In one village, the local police heard the helo force fly overhead and laid down all their weapons in the front of the police station. As the assault team entered the village, they were all standing at attention awaiting the opportunity to surrender to the Raven. The locals had heard how the PDF "got waxed" in the city, and they did not want to do battle with the Americans. They thought surrender was the better part of valor.

On one of these Eagle flights, old man Murphy struck again. After one Chinook landed on a drop zone in the middle of nowhere, the other Chinook flew directly overhead prior to landing next to it. As the Chinook over flew its partner, the downwash of the helicopter was so tremendous that it bent the rotor blades of the one sitting on the ground.

When word got back to me in the JOC, I had to organize a huge logistical effort to repair and recover the broken helicopter. We had to send maintenance troops, new blades, a crane, generators for power, and light carts to this remote location. It would take eighteen hours to accomplish the repairs, but we made it happen and the helicopter was fixed and returned to action. These Eagle flights continued for several days. That was the way Raven and I spent Christmas in Panama. I was providing helicopters, and he was walking around the countryside looking for Manny.

I had been eating MREs for eight days in the hangar and I remember for Christmas dinner we had T-rations of lasagna. These were big tin foil bins of prepackaged lasagna heated up over pans of boiling water. It was one of the worst meals I ever had, and having it on Christmas day made it even crummier. The fact that we hadn't found Noriega made the situation worse yet.

Later that Christmas night, a report came into the JOC that Noriega had somehow managed to avoid capture and went into exile in the Papal Nuncio. The Papal Nuncio was the Vatican's embassy in downtown Panama City.

The embassy was located in the fairly affluent Paitilla section of the city. In fact, it was very near the airfield where some brave Navy SEALs were killed in the process of destroying Noriega's private jet that was parked there. The aircraft could have been used by Noriega to leave the country. It was disabled by a well-placed rocket the first night to prevent such an event from happening. With no recourse or ability to escape, Noriega gave himself up to the Pope's emissary hoping for some kind of Christian redemption.

The Raven and his men were given orders to surround and secure the area. Raven moved his men into a Catholic girls' school across the street and set up his command post. In high-rise apartments that surrounded the area, he put snipers who could keep their eyes on Noriega and his movements inside the Papal Nuncio compound. A Holiday Inn was across and up the street a little way and the media moved in with all their cameras and microphones. With their modern technology, the media could pick up the orders Raven was sending out over his command radios. This "pissed off" the Raven, and he came up with an idea.

He asked for the Psychological Operations soldiers that were driving around the city to come to his location. The psyops troops were using their vehicles with mounted loudspeakers to tell the Panamanians to remain calm and off the streets until the situation was stabilized. The Raven had another use for the vehicles and loudspeakers.

He didn't want the media to know his intentions so he asked the commander if they could play some loud music to cover his radio commands. The commander said, "Sure," and gave the order to his soldiers to strategically set up their vehicles around the Papal Nuncio compound and let the music play. The soldiers were very young and broke out all the latest rock-and-roll tapes they had with them. For the next three days, non-stop rock-and-roll music was heard blaring from the loudspeakers.

Somehow the media misinterpreted this action as psychological warfare and that Raven was trying to mentally wear Noriega down. The media thought maybe Manny would eventually come out of the embassy compound after being driven insane by being kept up around the clock with good old-fashioned American rock-and-roll. This was not the case, however. It was just a ploy to provide operational security to the Raven's men and mask his intentions. Anyway, the music plan didn't work on Manny, but the number of complaints that came in from the local Panamanians ended the rock-and-roll chapter of the Panama invasion.

After three more days, another assault team relieved Raven and his men. Raven's men returned to the hangar, packed up all their gear and returned to Fort Bragg. Hawk was sent back also, since the tactical missions had come to an end. In less than two weeks, Hawk had coordinated 180 combat and combat support missions for all our forces in the field. It had been a pretty intense time, and again, it was thrilling to have been a part of the action.

The Hawk worked in the Operations Directorate of the headquarters which was known as the J3. Those of us who worked there all thought we were prima donnas and that the whole world revolved around us. We believed everyone else, including the Intelligence, Communications, Logistics, and Administration divisions, existed only to support the Operations Directorate. Because of this certain outlook, we were a very competitive bunch in the first place. We had personnel from all the disciplines of special operations warfare including Navy SEALS, Army Special Forces and Air Force commandos in the J3.

Embedded in the J3 was an exclusive air branch consisting of Army and Air Force pilots. Every last one of us was an alpha male! This competitive spirit was truly a great environment in which to work. We would razz each other mercilessly on a daily basis, but it was all in fun and jest. We were very thick-skinned, a necessity for survival in that environment. If you showed any sign of weakness or thin skin, you immediately became a target!

An Air Force fighter pilot was assigned to the Operations Directorate but to a different branch than the one where I worked. We didn't have much use for fighter aircraft back then, so he was sort of put in a back office and we forgot about him during the Just Cause operation. He stayed back in the rear and called wives, offering his help while we were gone. He would fix broken dishwashers or repair flat tires. He was very quiet and unassuming. He also had a terrific and irreverent sense of humor, as we would find out later.

After the Command returned from Panama, an intense young Major in the Intelligence Directorate wrote a letter to his people, thanking them for a job well done. This is what he had to say: "The last six months have been the most compressed and challenging period in the nine-year history of our command. Aside from normal requirements, we have actively engaged in Operations Blue Fork, Nimble Horse, Acid Weed, Poke Gambit, Nifty Box, Blue Knife, Polaroid Day, Poplar Forest, Trident Climber and the recently completed Just Cause. Throughout these operations, we never failed to provide timely and consistent intelligence support and recommendations to the Command and our forces in spite of the frustrations of no mission focus, single source intelligence reporting, deployments, missed holidays, etc. During this time we lost several critical team players and brought on board seven new, inexperienced men who were trained under crisis rather than normal on-the-job training. For this, you need to be proud of yourselves as individuals and collectively as a winning team.

"Unfortunately, as the new Commanding General stated during the change of command, 'Special Operations is our business and business is good.' I see no immediate relief from this compression as long as the insurgency in El Salvador continues; business remains lucrative for the cartel, there are coups in the Philippines, hostages being held in Lebanon, and whatever else.

"When we are pushed, as we have been, we occasionally 'bite' at each other and feel sorry for ourselves…human flaws that are more indicative of losers than winners. I include myself in this lot. Therefore I ask each of you to reach deep into your professional souls and continue to persevere as the winning team we are.

"You need to know, I'm more proud of being on the Intelligence team than any other team I've served with. We have done well and will continue to do well…just like that majestic swan on the lake who appears unruffled on the surface but under the water its powerful legs toil continuously without notice. We are those legs. Thanks, the Major"

This letter was posted on a bulletin board in the Intelligence Directorate. Two weeks later, it mysteriously showed up on the J3 bulletin board with a newer version attached to it. Only much later did we discover the identity of the author of this new document. It was our fighter pilot!

This was what the newer version said. "The last six months have been awesome. I mean really, if it hasn't been one thing it's been another. Every time you turn around some petty asshole in some festering pustule of a third world country gets a "hard-on" for the USA and we flinch responsively. Besides our morning physical training, executive lunches, staff calls at the Officers' Club, and flagrant abuse of the phones, we have been involved in Operations Blue Plate, Banner Savior, Musical Chairs, Banner Spoon, Spoon Savior, Acrid Smell, Illicit Sex, Tropical Boondoggle, Obscene Calls and God knows what-all we've forgotten about by the next morning.

"Sometimes the mission got done. But that's beside the point. We looked good in the shower, and our after-action reviews and hot washes have consistently drawn rave reviews. The real statistics speak for themselves... $82,000,000 in boondoggles and good deals are nothing to sneeze at.

"Throughout these operations we never failed to whine, whimper, snivel, and abuse those about us that were innocent of wrongdoing. When key personnel have been unable to complete a foursome while deployed, or when new guys with little previous experience at debauchery are forced to go on good deals to idyllic locations you heard some prime, grade A whining. When pushed we whine. Sometimes we're abusive. Most of the time we're horny. All are human flaws (well, mostly all) that can be overcome with a little discipline and will power. I don't see it happening any time soon, though.

"You heard the Commanding General say that 'Special Operations is our job…' What the General meant to say was, 'Let's get this change-of-command over and grab a brewskie.' Others of you didn't hear the Commanding General. Some of you aren't aware we have a new CG and some are curious what CG stands for. But that's beside the point.

"I'm proud of you guys. When the soap drops you're the first to bend over for it. Nowhere else will you see re-flexes like that. Like the fresh-fucked duck, our assholes may seem a bit tender, but it was an experience we'll not soon forget. And the world is just a little bit better for it all. But that's not important. Remember…keep your backs to the wall and your soap on a rope. Thanks, the Boss." I laughed my ass off reading the new version.

This is a small glimpse into the world of the Raven and the Hawk. When dealing in death and destruction, a little humor sometimes brings levity to our daily lives. I am sure it is much like the medical world.

A few days, after we returned to Fort Bragg, Noriega surrendered peacefully and was flown to Miami, Florida, to stand trial on numerous charges, including launder-ing millions of dollars in drug money. Manuel Noriega received a forty-five year prison sentence.

The Raven and the Hawk were victorious once again.

10 SCUD HUNTING

On August 6, 1990, Saddam Hussein's forces invaded Kuwait, smashed the Kuwaiti military and declared the country Iraq's nineteenth province. The United States reacted quickly and four days later, America's lumbering giant was rolling down the runway at Pope AFB, North Carolina. The 82nd Airborne Ready Brigade was flown to Saudi Arabia in case Saddam had further intentions. Although this brigade was considered no more than a speed bump at the time, there was no further movement by Iraqi forces beyond the Kuwaiti border.

After the Panamanian success story, the Hawk received orders to return to the big blue Air Force and fly the C-141 Starlifter again. The Hawk went to Altus AFB, Oklahoma in June, 1990 for a six-week refresher course and completed training in mid-July. During this time in Oklahoma, the Hawk was promoted to Lieutenant Colonel. I returned to Fort Bragg to out- process and move my family and household goods to Charleston AFB, South Carolina. I was going home after five years behind the "Green Door", as Special Operations is sometimes called.

After Iraq invaded Kuwait, my wife was sitting with me outside the Pope transient living facility, watching C-141 and C-5 aircraft landing and taking off every 30 minutes. The feeling of patriotism hung heavily in the air, which brought tears to my wife's eyes. The movement of the 82nd Airborne was in full swing, and I was stuck at Pope trying to clear quarters. The huge jets loaded with American soldiers and equipment lumbered into the blue Carolina sky headed for Saudi Arabia. I was thinking, "I'm gonna miss the fucking war!" Was I wrong, again.

The Hawk checked into Charleston on August 10, 1990, as a fully qualified pilot and was designated by the Squadron Commander as the Chief Pilot. I was put in charge of 77 young, full-of-piss-and-vinegar, snot-nosed pilots. What an exciting time to have that many pilots under my control.

A real world contingency was just in its infancy, and it was my responsibility to ensure that these young pilots would fly and fight as a cohesive unit. Pilots would continue to upgrade and train, although they would do so under wartime, rather than peacetime, conditions. The hours we flew would be nothing like we had ever experienced before. The aircrews would fly to some base in the United States and take on a full load of aircraft parts, Army personnel, tanks (I flew an Army Sheridan tank in the back of one of my aircraft), toilet paper, sodas, etc. You name it, we carried it.

The stuff would be flown eight hours to a base in Germany or Spain, and a new crew would then fly down to Saudi Arabia and back, which was 15 hours of flying, round trip. After 12 hours of rest, another round trip was flown. This continued until the aircrew racked up 150 hours of flight time, which was the maximum permissible during wartime flying conditions. In peacetime, a crewmember was not allowed to fly more than 125 hours a month.

Normally, an aircrew member was fortunate to accumulate an average of 50 hours of flight time in a month. I, personally, took off on 17 August and returned home 18 days later after 153 hours of flight time. (Maybe not a record, but close to it.) That was a staggering average of almost 10 hours a day of being airborne in the "aluminum tube" as we affectionately, or not so affectionately, called our C-141. I could not fly again for almost a month until my flight-time average had diminished sufficiently that I could start over again. This would go on for a solid six months as we moved the equivalent of Oklahoma City (approximately 500,000 people and all their belongings), lock, stock and barrel, to Southwest Asia.

Finally, in late January, 1991, President Bush ran out of patience and the air war commenced over Iraq. Called "Desert Storm" by General Norman Schwarzkopf, it would deliver the thunder and lightning he called for. With a non-stop, round-the-clock bombing effort, the need to deliver more ammunition, bombs, fuel and spare aircraft parts rose exponentially. The strategic airlift system was being stretched to the maximum, as were the aircrews. It was a testament to the Air Force system that only one aircraft was lost during this immense amount of intensive flying by our military pilots and aircrews, and that one loss was due to a mechanical failure.

I flew on Super Bowl Sunday and landed in Riyadh, Saudi Arabia. It was just like any other workday during Desert Storm. There was no place to watch or even listen to the game. Personnel were focused on unloading and refueling our aircraft as quickly as possible, so we could get back in the air to return to pick up another load.

As we waited for our aircraft to be refueled, the aircrew sat on the ramp and looked around the base. There were a number of Patriot missile batteries strategically placed around the airfield. These Patriots were the anti-missile missiles that were used quite effectively against the Scud missiles launched by Saddam Hussein's forces targeting Riyadh, Dhahran and Israel.

So why am I telling you all this? Well, the Hawk had been involved from just about the start of Desert Shield right on through the transition to Desert Storm. Periodically, I would call the Raven and see what he was up to. He was one frustrated son of a gun. There was no mission for his men so they remained at their home base continuing to train in their special-mission tasks.

Near the end of January, as I returned from my latest mission to Southwest Asia, I called my friend once again, but this time I did not get an answer at his office. I then called his wife to say hello and see if she knew where he was. She told me he had left a few weeks before, and she hadn't heard from him since. I did some more checking and was unable to find out where the Raven had gone. It wasn't until years later that I got the full story from my friend.

As the Scud missiles started to fall in and around Tel Aviv, Israel, the Israelis prepared to retaliate against Iraq. The coalition that would eventually crush the Iraqis had been carefully constructed and nurtured by President Bush and included numerous Arab countries. With the possible involvement of Israel, there was the potential of the coalition unraveling and the Arab nations realigning with Iraq against Israel. This called for some delicate negotiations with the Israelis.

As soon as the first Scud landed in Israel, the brainstorming began at U. S. National Command Authority, and a two-pronged defense of Israel was devised. Firstly, the United States would provide Patriot missile batteries at no cost to the Israelis, and secondly, a lethal force would be unleashed to hunt down and destroy the Scud launchers and missiles. This was a new form of terrorism. These missiles would land in civilian neighborhoods completely unannounced and bring instantaneous devastation and death. Only the screams of the dying could be heard. Who better to fight this new form of terrorism than America's most excellent counterterrorists, the Raven and his men? That was enough to pacify the Israelis and they never entered the war.

The orders swiftly came down to the Raven to deploy his men to Nellis AFB in Nevada. With this new mission, the Raven had to develop new tactics, techniques and procedures to conduct this direct- action mission, which is one of the core missions of Special Forces.

With helicopters, desert mobility vehicles and armed and dangerous men, the Raven trained in the Nevada desert for three weeks before being sent to Saudi Arabia. The intent of the Scud-hunting mission would be to find the launchers and destroy them. This would be accomplished by back tracking the flights of those missiles already launched. The trajectories and flight times would be put into an equation and the launch site position could then be extrapolated. Based on this information, circles were drawn on the map, which were nominally called Scud baskets. Under cover of darkness, the helicopters would fly Raven's men and vehicles as close to the launch site as possible without alerting the enemy. The men would then travel in their specially modified vehicles across the desert and search these Scud baskets for fixed or mobile Scud launchers.

If the site was fixed, a single radio call was made to an Airborne Warning and Control (AWAC) aircraft with the laser-designated coordinates of the site. An Air Force bomber mission was immediately launched against the site. The aircraft would then bomb the site back to the Stone Age! If the site was mobile, Raven and his men would attack the Scud convoy and destroy the launcher and support vehicles.

The Raven's first and last mission was deep into Western Iraq but it was another doozy! Launching from a site somewhere in Saudi Arabia, Raven and 23 of his men were cross-loaded into two MH-53s and two MH-47s. Packed into the bellies of the helicopters were two desert mobility vehicles and a HUMVEE, with enough fuel, ammunition, water and food for two weeks. Escorting the flight were two heavily-armed MH-60 Blackhawks. The flight was flown at night using NVGs and lasted about two hours. The flight was uneventful and the helicopters set down in the Iraqi desert in a place called Wadi Rutba, which was 35 KM south of Al Quyim. Al Quyim was a large military base in Western Iraq that was suspected of providing base support for the Scud launchers.

After offloading the vehicles and personnel, the helicopters departed and Raven and his men were situated deep behind enemy lines. Their plan was to move north toward Al Quyim and find a hide-site to hole up in until the next night. The team set off and drove across the desert nearly 20 miles north before finding a dry riverbed (wadi in Arabic) that would provide some cover.

After positioning the vehicles, the men draped camouflage netting over them. A recon team was posted 1,000 meters away in another wadi. The men then settled down to get some rest and tried to stay warm. It was February and the frigid desert night was nearly as cold as a freezing meat locker. During the night, Raven saw two Scud launches from their hide site. The launches into the black velvety sky of the desert night lit the place up like the Fourth of July.

At 10:00 o'clock the next morning, an Iraqi water truck drove by the hide-site, approximately 500 meters away. The truck suddenly stopped, the driver got out and looked in the general direction of the hide-site for about five minutes. Obviously, something caught the driver's attention or didn't look the same as the last 50 to 100 times he had driven by the site. He then got back into his truck and drove off.

Raven, sensing the potential seriousness of the situation, decided to move the team. The main body loaded up into the vehicles and headed south in broad daylight while the recon team was left behind. About 15 miles south, the brave warriors found a new hide-site and set up a defensive perimeter. A two-man observation post (OP) was situated on a nearby hill. The men's adrenaline was pumping like mad and their senses were at a heightened awareness. They would need it!

The water truck driver must have actually seen something amiss when driving by their position earlier and reported it to someone at the base. Around four o'clock in the afternoon, the OP reported a convoy of vehicles headed their way. An armored mechanized company of 80 Iraqi soldiers was tracking the Scud hunters. The hunters had become the hunted. This was nothing new for the Raven. It was Vietnam fucking all over again!

In the lead of the Iraqi convoy were three armored vehicles, followed by two troop-carrier trucks. The convoy pulled up to some sand dunes only 300 meters away. As the convoy got closer, the lead vehicle opened up with a 12.7mm-machine gun into the OP site. One of Raven's men was shot through the ankle. Raven's men responded with their Mark 19s, .50-caliber and 7.62 .60-cal machine guns, which were mounted on the desert mobility vehicles. Two of the lead vehicles were immediately destroyed. The Iraqi soldiers dismounted their troop trucks and returned small arms' fire while others launched rocket propelled grenades (RPGs). Raven counted a total of six RPGs fired at their position, but every one of them overshot its mark. The firing by Raven's men was so intense that the Iraqis could not get off a determined shot. They were just shooting wildly at the Raven's hide-site.

When Raven received word that one of his men was wounded at the OP, he dispatched one of his vehicles toward their position. The vehicle couldn't make it, so one guy ran to the OP and carried the wounded man back to the vehicle. Under withering enemy fire, he miraculously escaped injury. This soldier later received a Silver Star for his actions.

As the sun set and the sky turned purple, the Americans made their break. The three vehicles hightailed it across the desert and didn't stop, traveling thirty kilometers to the south. After setting up their radios and a defensive position, Raven called for an emergency extraction. A pair of Blackhawks picked up the recon team that the Raven had left behind at the original hide-sites. The MH-53s and MH-47s flew to the Raven's new position and uploaded the vehicles and his men.

On the return flight, the Raven sat inside a MH-47 with the ramp down and observed a missile launched at the aircraft. Luckily the missile missed but as it flew by, the interior of the aircraft was lit up like the lights coming on at the movie theater. Raven thought he was done for!

The heavily armed Blackhawks flying escort duty immediately went into action. Those pilots' eyes must have been as big as moon pies, and they started salivating like rabid dogs as they launched wave after wave of 2.75 rockets and fired their miniguns into the missile launch-site. The tracers from the 7.62 machine guns were like a continuous stream of fireworks. The site was wiped out and the flight made it to their home base without further incident.

Soon after this Scud-hunting mission was completed, an unfortunate American friendly-fire incident occurred. The battalion commander of an Apache unit mistakenly fired upon a Bradley mechanized unit and American soldiers were killed. An order was immediately published to keep all battalion commanders from front-line fighting positions. The thought was that not all battalion commanders were as proficient in combat-fighting skills as the young men under their command, who trained all the time. In order to prevent another potential friendly-fire incident, only company commanders and below would do the fighting. The battalion commander would remain behind and command his forces from the headquarters.

As a result, the Raven was forced to stay at their Saudi staging base and send his men out on the Scud-hunting missions without him. A warrior kept locked up like a cat in a cage was an unhealthy situation for the Raven. Rumor has it that he became sullen and ornery with his superiors. Ultimately, it almost cost him the command of the unit he loved so dearly. After too many run-ins with his boss, he was delayed taking command of the unit for two years.

The Raven and his men conducted the Scud-hunting missions in western Iraq for six weeks. The results were somewhat mixed. Only one Scud launcher was confirmed destroyed. However, the Iraqis were alerted to the fact that somebody dangerous was operating in their own backyard, which prevented them from using their pre-surveyed launch sites. After altering their launch positions, the notably inaccurate Scuds began to over-shoot and land in the Mediterranean Sea or come up short and land harmlessly in the Negev desert, rather than downtown Tel Aviv.

Intelligence sources reported that the Iraqis believed the intruders were Israelis. I am not sure if any of Raven's men were Jewish, but the final result was a resounding success. The Israelis stayed out of the fight, the coalition remained in place and Saddam Hussein's military was thoroughly decimated in the ensuing 100-hour ground war. It was reported that 300,000 Iraqis lost their lives in Desert Storm. The Raven and the Hawk played their small parts in this war and were rewarded with another victory against tyranny to notch in their respective belts.

11 "THE MOG"

Somalia was another fucking hellhole that the Hawk swore God forgot about. God was leaving it up to human beings to make something of this forsaken land, and they were failing miserably.

Somalia, before the infamous *Blackhawk Down* incident, was an incredibly rewarding experience, both personally and professionally for the Hawk. Instead of being a death deliverer as he had been for the last five years of his military career, the Hawk now had an opportunity to be a lifesaver. What a huge change of concept from what the Raven and Hawk had been involved with in the past. Ultimately, he was fucking wrong again!

The Hawk and the Raven were both able to command at the squadron/battalion level during contingency situations. It is the purest form of command when able to lead men in combat or peacekeeping operations. It is the closest you will ever be to troops in the field because as you become more senior in the military, the further distanced from troops you become.

The focus of senior military commanders and leaders becomes a numbers and money game. The number of troops you are responsible for, the number of training days for those troops and the amount of money for new equipment necessary to keep the troops combat-ready as frontline fighters and warriors. This was the Hawk's turn to experience combat-type scenarios up close and personal.

The Hawk's Change of Command ceremony was a glorious affair, rich with tradition and symbolism. The ceremony was conducted on August 11, 1992 and the opening speaker was the Squadron Operations officer who read the following:

"From ancient times, Armies throughout the world conducted ceremonies to commemorate victory over the enemy, to honor comrades-in-arms and to celebrate special occasions such as the change of command. History reveals that in the Middle Ages, it was not uncommon for the soldiers in the field to be unaware of who their commanders were or what they looked like. Formal changes of command afforded these troops the opportunity to witness the proceedings and actually see their commanders. The Continental Army of the United States conducted the first official ceremonies in America. This is the basis from which the present ceremony is derived. Today, the primary purpose of the Change of Command is to allow the subordinates to witness the formal transfer of total responsibility, authority and accountability from one officer to another. These ceremonies have added color and pageantry to military life while preserving tradition stimulating esprit de corps."

The Group Commander then provided the following commentary:

"We are about to go through a ceremony that won't take very long, but it's a ceremony steeped in tradition and important to the life of an organization, especially an organization like the Airlift Control Squadron, because it's symbolic of growth, of movement, of life in an organization.

"I have evidence that other people besides me have recognized the Hawk's excellence and I'd like to read a letter from one of them:

On behalf of the Air Mobility Command's senior leadership, congratulations on your selection to command. We place great confidence in your ability to lead and make tough decisions. Our most fundamental charge as commanders is to ensure that our organizations are fit for combat, which includes efficient use of resources and retaining good people. Your people will look to you for exemplary leadership, motivation and common sense management. Take this special opportunity to identify top performers and develop their talents. Your effectiveness will be critically important as you begin your new command tour. I wish you and your wife every success in one of the most demanding and rewarding assignments of your career.

"That's signed General H.G. Johnson, Commander-in-Chief of Air Mobility Command. So, congratulations on that. I had the fortunate opportunity to be with General

Johnson last week when he was talking to Operations Group Commanders and one of the things that he said was, 'You might think that running the operations of your Wing is the most important part of your job, and you might think that leadership is the most important part of your job, but what is the most important part of your job is command.' And here is your letter straight from the same man saying that he's charging you to command the way that he would like you to, the way we all need. Let's now perform the official duties."

The Operations officer then called me, the outgoing Commander and the flag bearer forward and read the following words:

"Ladies and Gentlemen, the change of command ceremony will now begin with the reading of Air Force special order number G155. Under the provisions of Air Force regulation number 35-54, Lt. Col. (name withheld) assumes command of the 437th Airlift Control Squadron vice Lt. Col. Skip, effective 11 August 1992." (The squadron's banner was passed from the outgoing Commander to the Hawk as this was being read.)

The Hawk then proceeded to the podium and took the opportunity to deliver the following speech:

"Thank you, distinguished guests, friends and family. As a Squadron Commander, I feel like I just received my own gold medal. It's an honor and an opportunity that I've been preparing for, for a long time. And the time is at hand. I think back to the many people who have helped me along this path to command, and I wish I could thank every one of them personally. However small or large a part they played in bringing this command to fruition, this ceremony is as much for them as it is for me.

To the men and women of the 76th, your loyalty and support these past two years have been truly rewarding. It was a privilege to have served by your side during Desert Shield and Desert Storm. When I came into the squadron, I looked up, and there was a sign above the door, and the words read, "To Fly, To Fight, and To Win." These words reflect the determination and dedication that you possess. And I salute you.

To the men and women of the Airlift Control Squadron, you also have a rich and proud heritage. Normally, you are the first in and last out. Your performance during the Persian Gulf War is a legacy for others to remember. I received my squadron patch the other day, and I looked at the words and it said on the bottom of the patch, "We Lead, So Others May Follow." This means, to me, being at the tip of the spear. I couldn't have asked for a better location.

I want to thank the leadership of this Wing for challenging me with this command. On this incredible day, my final thought comes from a passage in the Bible. I quote from Isaiah, Chapter Six, Verse Eight, and it reads, 'And the Lord said, 'Who shall I send and Who shall go forth', then said I 'Here am I, send me'. Thank you and God Bless America."

The tip of the spear - first in, last out - so others may follow. How was I to know how prophetic I would truly be!

The Hawk was now an Airlift Control Squadron Commander. For those not familiar with an Airlift Control Squadron, it is a mini-Air Force base with all the functions represented. This mini-base can be packed up, transported half-way around the world, unpacked, built up and operated around-the-clock in a bare-base environment.

The Commander has operational control of up to 400 personnel trained in all spectrums of strategic and tactical airlift operations. These airlift support operations personnel include cargo handlers, passenger manifesting specialists, aircraft mechanics, fuel handlers, security police, ramp coordinators, weathermen, mission planners, chaplains, medics and the list goes on and on.

This tutorial is provided because the Hawk's unit facilitated the first American forces deployed in support of Operation Provide Relief, the humanitarian mission to feed the starving Somali population.

What started as a beautiful, moving experience went fucking horribly wrong and became one of the nation's darkest moments in recent years. The initial intent was to go to Somalia and defeat starvation.

Tribal animosities, dating back who knows how long, erupted in 1991 with the overthrow of Somalia's dictator, Mohammed Siad Barre. By the summer of 1992, the world was seeing pictures of children's bloated bellies, sunken eyes and flies feasting on lifeless faces and bodies. As these gruesome sights were splashed all over television, then-President Bush and the American people decided they had seen enough. The Hawk had been in command all of eight days when the orders came.

In August, 1992, the Hawk and many others were sent to Mombasa, Kenya to commence the battle called

Operation Provide Relief.

Trying to explain how that victory was achieved is quite easy. When awakening the huge American military-industrial complex, America does it right. American know-how, technology and the will-to-win drove us to an overwhelming victory. The United States commenced with an enormous logistical undertaking requiring ships, planes and personnel.

The food arrived by ship at Mombasa's seaport, was downloaded to large Kenyan trucks, and driven to Moi International Airport. This mission required the use of fourteen C-130 aircraft that would fly two shuttles a day from Moi to unimproved dirt-strips in Somalia at Baidoa, Oddur, and Baledogle. These round-trip flights lasted four hours and transported six pallets of food per aircraft. Each pallet was built up by hand before departing Mombasa and weighed 7500 pounds. It was subsequently dismantled by hand upon arrival at these dirt-strip airfields, and the food was loaded onto trucks to be driven to distribution centers.

Although the mission lasted for only three months, it took quite a toll on the aircraft, crews and support personnel who worked these flights of mercy.

As a consequence, the cost became much too prohibitive. The wear and tear on the planes, and the constant rotation of people, who were quartered in five-star hotels on the beaches of Mombasa (which was a large European tourist destination and impacted on the tourism industry of Kenya) contributed to the next strategic move in the war on starvation.

President Bush, on the advice of his staff, determined

that Operation Provide Relief had become an overly expensive effort and the decision was made to shutdown the operation. The Hawk's squadron was redeployed to its home base in late October, 1992.

The reprieve at home was short-lived as we subsequently and almost immediately deployed to Griffiss AFB, New York in early December, 1992 to facilitate the deployment of the soldiers of the U.S. Army's 10th Mountain Division. The President had decided to send the 1st Marine Division and the 10th Mountain Division to secure the Mogadishu airport and seaport facilities, respectively.

This effort was named Operation Restore Hope and was a huge undertaking. A benign invasion of Somalia was planned and executed in December, 1992. Pictures flooded television screens as CNN, already in place on the beach, filmed wide-eyed, disbelieving Navy SEALs as they crossed the beaches of Mogadishu, Somalia's beleaguered and war-torn capital. The SEALs were poised and prepared for battle only to be met by American television crews as the opposing hostile force.

By securing the seaport, large cargo ships could transport huge quantities of food straight to Somalia along with the vehicles needed to carry it throughout the country. Additionally, vehicles to carry the Army soldiers and Marines and their weapons for protection of the food convoys were needed. Upon securing the two main embarkation facilities, the Marines and Army moved out, securing the rest of the country that was in the hands of feuding warlords and their loyal factions. This was a country in total anarchy with no central government at the time of the American-led intervention. There were no gas stations along the roads, no McDonalds to grab a burger and fries, no electrical power and no clean water (nor any kind of water, for that matter) in this drought-stricken country.

The huge convoys had to be self-sufficient as they drove to the far reaches of the country. Since Somalia is as big as the state of California in size and length, this was a huge undertaking. Fuel farms and water purifying units were built. Water and fuel tankers had to accompany the convoys in order to keep the vehicles running.

In less than three weeks, from December 6th to December 24th, 17,000 American Marines and 10th Mountain Division Army soldiers were delivered to Somalia and proceeded to spread out over the entire countryside. It took less than a month to complete this phase, and on Christmas Day, 1992, the Commanding General, Marine LTG Johnson declared victory.

The Hawk's unit completed the deployment of the 10th Mountain Division's equipment in mid-January, 1993 and returned home. My hardworking, under-rested squadron was just catching its collective breath, completing much-needed maintenance on our equipment when the next call came. The unit was ordered to deploy to Mogadishu in early March, 1993 and relieve their sister unit from Germany, which had been on the ground since early December and was on the receiving end of the forces deploying into Somalia.

Upon arrival, the Hawk's squadron re-acclimated and

took its place among the nearly 28,000 American and coalition forces in country. It then became the Hawk's responsibility to start the reverse process. The squadron commenced the redeployment of American forces to the U.S., while receiving Pakistani and other allied forces as the United Nations began to establish its foothold in the country. By the time the Hawk's unit was rotated out in late May 1993, the American presence had been reduced to 4,000 personnel.

Only a few months later, the American people were seeing the awful pictures, and journalists were writing columns about "the nation-building debacle in Somalia" and the "terrible slaughter of U.S. Army Rangers in the streets of Mogadishu." This historical picture does not tell the complete story.

The Hawk was successfully released from command of his squadron after only one year. The unit had spent seven months of it deployed in the field in the harshest possible conditions. Winter was spent in up-state New York near Lake Erie with the effects of lake front snow storms, severe cold and icing conditions. The spring was spent in sweltering tents, 500 meters from the Mogadishu runway. The noise, blowing sand and dust from landing and departing aircraft forced us to wear ear and eye protection constantly.

Though the conditions were dreadful, this was probably the best year of the Hawk's life. He was a commander of troops in the field supporting real-world operations. He never had the opportunity to train or exercise. Every day, the unit was accomplishing the mission that they would normally train and exercise for if they were in garrison.

The dedicated efforts of the squadron paid huge benefits on discipline and morale as well. The unit had a member with a DUI conviction, a member being retired for serious medical problems and another one facing a UCMJ action for conduct unbecoming an NCO. In the one year of sustained activities, there were absolutely zero disciplinary problems and morale soared as the professional men and women of the unit sought to make a difference in the world. The squadron personnel were very focused and worked feverishly around-the-clock in support of the Somali effort.

Some of the remarkable scenes that remain vivid in Hawk's mind even to this day were poignant testaments to nation-building.

He remembers an airport hangar full of young airmen on break from building pallets, loading planes or fixing them, lying on stretchers. They were voluntarily giving blood by the pint to our host country's hospitals in Mombasa, which was suffering from an AIDS epidemic.

He remembers landing at an airfield and driving to a Somali refugee camp and seeing the fruits of their labors paying off as supplies were being delivered. Healthy Somali children were playing and upon spotting U.S. personnel in uniform, immediately surrounded them and thanked them for their help.

He recalls going on a medical capabilities operation (MEDCAP) with a convoy of soldiers and medics. They went into the Somali countryside, visiting a village and providing medical and health care treatment to the indigenous population. The people were sick and fighting among themselves to see the few doctors available. The soldiers had to maintain order so the doctors could do their jobs. After a full day of dispensing medicine, water and food to the people, the Americans all felt morally uplifted on their drive back to Mogadishu.

The Hawk read an article that soldiers were holding English and reading classes for the Somali children, who no longer had any schools to attend.

A final scene which played out repeatedly in his mind was the time the Hawk and ten of his men, armed to the teeth, ventured into downtown Mogadishu on a drive from the airport to the seaport. They stopped momentarily to survey the enormous damage inflicted on the city's infrastructure. Banks, government buildings, even mosques, were bullet-riddled and burned-out shells. A poor, young Somali boy approached the vehicles, and a young airman that worked for the Hawk threw a bag of Skittles candy to the child. The kid caught the bag, gave the airman a thumb's up and had a beautiful smile on that ebony face, one that could light up a night sky.

The Hawk feels sure the Americans who served in the Somali effort played out many other scenes like this. The main point he wishes for the American people to realize is that starvation in Somalia was defeated and that many soldiers, sailors, marines and airmen played key roles in that victory.

A nation cannot even begin to attempt to function if the population is decimated by famine. As an outgrowth of the war on starvation, these great servicemen successfully carried out many nation-building operations. They performed their skills during a contingency situation, which they had been training for since they joined the services. They accomplished this by protecting convoys from the Somali "Road Warrior" vehicles known as "technicals", conducting medical clinics, and restoring the airport and seaport, which had been devastated by war, to an operational status. This was the best kind of training our soldiers could ever receive.

The Hawk doesn't know how the national strategy went awry that led to the firefight which killed those 18 Americans in October, 1993, but it surely detracted from the tremendous amount of positive progress that had been made to that point.

The "MOG" was a defining point in the Hawk's military career. It was a dichotomy of mixed emotions. On the one hand, people's lives were being saved; on the other, after restoring their health, they disintegrated into fanatical, mob-mentality, American-hating tribal factions.

The country of Somalia doesn't really exist. To this day, there is no government, no police department, no national army, no banks, nor any justice system. Somalia is just an anomaly of the world, a God-forsaken part of the planet that even America couldn't save!

12 TRAVELS WITH BIG RED

As the General's car slowed for early morning traffic in a certain Middle Eastern capital, two motorcycles with a driver and rider each easily maneuvered their way closer. As the motorcycles approached the vehicle, the riders jumped off the bikes, pulled submachine guns from under their jackets and fired at point-blank range into the car. The vehicle's driver, bodyguards and the General were instantly slaughtered, their bodies riddled with bullets. Bloody shards of glass and pieces of human flesh were splattered everywhere over the interior of the car. After completing their grisly act, the shooters got back on the motorcycles and sped away, disappearing into the traffic as they weaved their way to escape.

Big Red always had the Hawk sit in the back seat while he sat up front with the driver as we traveled around the Middle East. Big Red was the Commanding General of a Special Operations Command with responsibility for most of the Arab world, part of Africa and South Asia. The

Hawk had been assigned to his staff, but the command was too small for the General to have an aide assigned. My superior selected me to be the General's executive officer. My job was to coordinate his travels to these distant lands and to accompany him on these trips of national importance.

One day I asked why he had me sit in the back with himself up front, when it was common courtesy to have the VIP sit in the back. The General turned to me and said, "That's exactly what the bad guys think, so if we get ambushed, they will think you are the person of importance and take you out!" Not a comforting thought, but I really liked Big Red, and for some reason we hit it off.

He was a rather large, chain-smoking, red-faced and red-haired Irishman, who enjoyed knocking back a shot or two of Scotch whisky every now and then. He gave me valuable lessons in the history and knowledge of the Middle East as well as life in general. This was a man who on the long flights from our base in Florida to the Middle East (which took almost 15 hours of flying) would read *Diplomacy* by Henry Kissinger for "light reading." I was reading Tom Clancy action and adventure novels. If I read one page of *Diplomacy*, I would have been asleep before I got to page two.

Big Red graduated from the Citadel, spent his early formative years as a Green Beret, served in Vietnam and then decided to get his Master's degree in Anthropology from Syracuse University. The U.S. Army, in its infinite wisdom, decided he needed to teach, so he spent a tour doing just that at West Point.

He then went back to Special Forces and commanded

at the battalion and group levels. Somewhere he found time to go to the Strategic Studies Institute instead of the Army War College for his Senior Level Staff School.

As Big Red completed his Senior Level School, President Carter brokered a peace deal between Egypt and the U.S. ally, Israel. The picture on the cover of all the major magazines of Anwar Sadat, Menachem Begin and Jimmy Carter in a three-way handshake symbolized the peace treaty, which still lasts to this day.

This peace treaty came with a cost associated, although it was mostly monetary and military hardware in nature. During the 1973 War, the Egyptian Army had been completely decimated by the Israeli Defense Forces (IDF). Therefore, as part of the deal, the Egyptians would receive $3 billion dollars a year in modern United States military equipment. A bunch of that money was earmarked to re-arm and modernize the Egyptian Army with U.S.-built Abrams tanks.

Big Red was given the responsibility to order, purchase, procure, and deliver the tanks to the Egyptian Army. As the old saying goes, "the devil is always in the details," and Big Red was good at details. Carter negotiated the peace, but Big Red made sure it actually happened. Much later, those Abrams tanks were used in the first Gulf War as Egypt joined the coalition to oust Saddam Hussein's forces from Kuwait. This was a major detail of the peace treaty that had to be performed by some unknown person until one day you actually meet that person and find out the real story behind the peace!

According to Clausewitz, the military is an extension

of government policy or politics; a way to possibly influence another country. There is a saying that politics and religion make strange bedfellows, but I believe the military and politics make even stranger ones.

The first real adventure for the Hawk, while traveling with Big Red, occurred in the Horn of Africa. A visit to the newly-independent country of Eritrea was planned. The itinerary for the Hawk and Big Red as we headed to Eritrea included stops along the way in Kenya and Ethiopia.

The first stop was in Nairobi, Kenya, and was highlighted by our stay in the Safari Lodge. It was on the outskirts of Nairobi, but it was where the General insisted on staying when the Hawk put the trip together. After we checked in, we both unpacked and then met in the hotel bar. As I ordered a cocktail to unwind from the 15-hour flight, the Hawk learned the significance of this particular hotel. Kenya was where the famous American author, Ernest Hemingway, spent time big-game hunting in the early 1930s. Hemingway then became ill and recovered his health in this same hotel. The idea for the book, *The Snows of Kilimanjaro*, published in 1938, originated in this very same hotel as he was recovering. Big Red knew this and only shared it with me upon our arrival. It was another of those small but interesting facets of getting to travel our AOR (area of responsibility).

The purpose of our visit to Kenya was to meet and conduct talks with the U. S. Ambassador. She greeted us wearing a native kaftan. We would need her approval for Army Special Forces soldiers to travel to Kenya and train

Kenyan soldiers in the discipline of peacekeeping. She would be instrumental in eventually convincing the host government, through her official contacts, that this training would be very beneficial to the host nation.

As part of the United States strategic political plan, armed forces from several countries on the African continent needed to be capable of responding to regional "hotspots", civil wars, political upheaval and unrest, or a nation's complete breakdown into anarchy. This policy was labeled the African Crisis Response Proposal. African nations would provide the soldiers, but they needed to be specifically trained in peacekeeping duties. Army Special Forces would train battalions from several nations which, in times of crisis, could be deployed to the country in turmoil to provide security and peacekeeping.

Peacekeeping duties included the use of non-lethal weapons, riot-control techniques, military operations in urban environment training (MOUT), patrolling, etc. Special Forces soldiers could provide all of this training. One of the core missions of the Army's Green Berets was FID (pronounced just like it looks), the acronym for Foreign Internal Defense.

The bottom line was money. Big Red knew that training for our Special Forces was supported by many different "cash cows" as he called them, and he was a genius in procuring that money. The Hawk not only got to travel and "grip and grin" with the famous and near-famous, but he also received an education in fiscal responsibility, regional history and politics.

Large amounts of money were allocated to the ACRP

in order to allow other countries to send their troops to the hostile area. The United States civilian leadership believed that having soldiers from the African countries deployed to hotspots, where troops could be exposed to danger and potential fatalities, was better than having young American soldiers vulnerable.

It was actually a win-win situation all around. Our Special Forces soldiers were able to deploy to countries in our AOR, stay for weeks to months at a time, and provide real-world training in tactics, organization, weapons familiarity, etc. In return, our troops would be exposed to the different cultures, environments, languages and social mores of some of the countries that they might possibly be deployed to in a real-world crisis. We would get American soldiers exposed to actual jungle, mountain, and desert training in just about every kind of harsh environment one can think of in Africa. Uncle Sugar would pay for it all. It was truly great training for our soldiers.

The country in crisis would win by having the neighboring countries' soldiers, who looked alike, acted alike and sounded alike, help stabilize their situation. The opportunity to cement friendly relationships between the countries' governments and militaries was another potential benefit.

So everybody won and Big Red was the purveyor of this news to the ambassador. She would convince the host nation to let American soldiers come to Kenya, provide the training to Kenya's army, and have Kenya sign up to be a country willing to provide a battalion (600 soldiers) in a crisis. Upon completion of the briefing and approval by the ambassador, the Hawk and Big Red flew on to Addis Ababa, Ethiopia.

The objective here was to provide the Ethiopians with de-mining training. At the height of the Ethiopian-Eritrean civil war, a million land mines had been planted along the major frontlines of battle. Now that the war was over, the international community, through the efforts of the late Princess Diana of Great Britain, looked at the mines as a grave humanitarian crisis.

A United Nations de-mining proposal became the prelude to a program specifically designed to try and remove these lethal and harmful land mines from places all over the world (Cambodia, Angola, Namibia, Eritrea, Ethiopia, Sri Lanka). The United States signed on to this plan and provided money to the program.

Big Red, in another of his psychic wisdoms, looked at the de-mining program as another opportunity to deploy Army SF and PSYOPS (Psychological Operations) soldiers to an area of the world they had not been exposed to before. The soldiers would practice their own skills by training host nation forces in de-mining methods, alerting the local populace to the dangers of mines, plotting the location of the mine fields, removing the mines, and eventually making the land a safe place for all to live. Making the area safe would allow the local inhabitants to stop worrying about a mine blowing up an innocent child while playing nearby or causing the loss of other lives or limbs. It would also increase the area of land available for growing crops, always an issue in famine-prone regions of Africa.

The final stop of our journey was Asmara, the capital of Eritrea, which sits on the top of a mountain plateau 7700 feet above sea level. Asmara is a beautiful, modern cosmopolitan city with many tree-lined avenues. The architecture of the buildings reflected the influence of the Italians, who defeated Ethiopia in a prelude to the start of World War II.

The host government officials that met us at the airport registered us in a hotel that was once the summer palace of His Imperial Majesty, the late Haile Selassie. Selassie, whose early legacy of Ethiopian pride and sovereignty, transformed Ethiopia into a major struggle between the old and new Colonial orders of the Dark Continent. In some places he was revered as a god, and in others he was representative of the corrupt leaders of the newly independent countries of Africa. Selassie was overthrown by a military coup in 1974 and died a year later.

Eritrea was awarded to Ethiopia in 1952 as part of a federation. Ethiopia annexed Eritrea ten years later, which sparked a 30-year civil war that ended in 1991, after Eritrean rebels fought and defeated Ethiopian governmental forces. Independence was subsequently approved overwhelmingly in a 1993 referendum.

The fight for independence was a lot like the American Civil War, except with a different outcome. Prior to the war, all of the soldiers were in the same army. Many of the men who became the leaders and commanders of the Eritrean rebels learned their skills while serving as members in the Ethiopian Army. The commanders were actually quite young (early twenties) when the war started, and by the time they tasted the fruits of victory they were still in their early forties.

After their victorious outcome, these same individuals found themselves in positions of power and were now running the country. They swapped their ragtag Army uniforms for three-piece suits and were now in charge. However, being fairly young still and holding powerful government positions was not a detriment to their Western-leaning ideals. When Big Red and I were taken by the U. S. embassy officials to meet them at a local restaurant, we were in for a pleasant surprise.

The Eritrean Secretary of Defense was a man named Petros Solomon. He was a thinly-built, handsome man with an infectious smile constantly etched on his face. I could understand why the rebels followed him as one of their commanders.

He was a people person and I suspected his men loved him and would readily die for him. Solomon was fond of Scotch whiskey, which made him and Big Red instant friends. I was purposely seated next to the Eritrean Air Force Chief of Staff. He had been sent to Russia for his flight training and was a former fighter pilot in the Ethiopian Air Force, flying MIG 21s.

When the civil war broke out, he told me that he deserted from the Ethiopian Air Force and returned to his Eritrean roots where he was born. When he walked into the restaurant that night, he was wearing a brown leather jacket with a fur-lined collar and cool, black Ray-Ban aviator sunglasses! Being pilots, we hit it off right away and after a few drinks, he shared with me his secrets. He had an attraction for Janet Jackson and enjoyed listening to the music of her brother, Michael.

Although dinner was supposed to be a social occasion, Big Red was able to conduct business between shots of Scotch. Part of the settlement between Ethiopia and the newly-created country of Eritrea was an agreement to allow Ethiopia to use Eritrea's main seaport, Massawa. With Eritrea's independence, Ethiopia had become a landlocked country and Eritrea borders on the Red Sea. Eritrea would allow Ethiopia to utilize Massawa to ship and receive goods from around the world. In addition, Massawa would make Eritrea an economically viable country, but the port facilities were in desperate need of repairs. As part of Ethiopia's strategy during the war, a ship loaded with ammunition and explosives was sunk in the main harbor.

A rather large amount of international funding was available to the Eritrean government for reconstruction purposes. The money would be used to repair and help restore the country's infrastructure damaged by the war. Our purpose was to convince the Eritrean government to allow United States military personnel to remove this ship and its' dangerous cargo from the ports' waters.

Big Red wanted to make use of this pot of money to deploy Navy SEALs, who would conduct underwater hydrographic surveys of the port. These surveys would provide the details and information necessary to exactly pinpoint the position of the ship and determine how to salvage it and the cargo. Information gained could have the dual purpose of use in a potential combat-type scenario. After all, the countries had just finished a civil war and were not on too-friendly terms. The very real possibility existed for another war, which actually occurred from 1998 to 2000.

After many rounds of drinks and a happy buzz in our heads, the General and I were brought back to our hotel. The next day we met with the President of Eritrea and again explained our purpose. He must have already been briefed by Petros Solomon because he quickly and wholeheartedly agreed to our proposition. The rest of the day, Big Red and I nursed our hangovers and took a small tour of the city.

The next morning we were picked up by an embassy driver and driven to the airport. As we approached the airport terminal, which was fairly small, we noticed hardly any activity. Our flight was scheduled to take us to Addis Ababa, where we would connect to a major carrier that would fly us to Europe on our way home to Florida. We remained in the car as the driver went into the terminal. He quickly returned and gave us the word that our flight had been cancelled. This was not good news as our connections were all dependant on us getting to Addis Ababa and making that international flight.

The embassy driver quickly made a phone call to the liaison officer, who had arranged our official visit and meetings. He told us to standby as he worked the problem. A short while later, the officer called us back and told us to remain at the airport. He had found a remedy to our situation and would link up with us there with the new arrangements.

When the liaison officer arrived at the airport, he had another individual in the car with him. It was my new buddy, the Eritrean Air Force Chief of Staff. Word had somehow been relayed to him about our dilemma and he came to our rescue. In his fleet of planes was a Chinese-made YAK 12, which was a small prop-driven aircraft. He was checked out as a pilot in it and volunteered his services to fly us to Addis in order to make our connecting flight. Big Red and I looked at each other, smiled and gave him a big thumbs up!

In less than an hour, the three of us were flying across the Great Rift Valley and looking at some of the most desolate but beautiful terrain I had ever seen. If we had had some kind of aircraft malfunction and crash-landed in this part of the world, I don't think we would have ever been found. However, the flight went uneventfully and we landed in Addis with time to spare to make our connection. After unloading our baggage, we thanked our distinguished pilot and went to shake his hand. To our surprise we received a bill for the gas! Traveling throughout what were considered third-world countries, I always carried spare cash from the Command's coffers and was able to pay him straightaway. In certain circumstances, the money was justified for dealing with the unknowns that sometimes reached out and bit us in the ass. In all honesty, it was a small price to pay for a trip to keep my busy General on schedule.

Three countries, three "cash cows", and wins for a lot of people; all accomplished on a twelve-day whirlwind tour.

Big Red, because of his position, was able to influence

and represent American strategic policy. The Hawk was allowed to watch, listen, learn and eventually chronicle these seemingly small events which seemed none-too-significant at the time, but proved in the long term to be extremely important and worthwhile.

When Big Red and the Hawk traveled to all these countries in Southwest Asia and the Horn of Africa, visas were required for entry into and out of each nation visited. The standard way of getting the visas was to send an Administrative Clerk to Washington, DC, who would spend a day going to each embassy with the General's and the Hawk's passports and obtaining the requisite visas for the trip planned. Not being an expert on visas, the Hawk just assumed that the passports were ready to go.

Unknown to the Hawk, there were actually different kinds of visas. There was a one-time entry and a multiple-entry type for the United Arab Emirates. On this particular trip, this visa SNAFU (situation normal, all fucked up) raised its ugly head. It seems as though the Hawk had been issued a multiple-entry visa and the General had a one-time entry visa in his passport.

The trip started with a flight into Abu Dhabi, where the UAE's special operations headquarters was located. After our visit was completed we flew on to Muscat, Oman, for a visit with the Omani Special Forces. After completing this portion of the trip, we were scheduled to fly to Jordan for a meeting with Prince Abdullah, Jordan's Special Forces commander. The Hawk always built extra days into the itinerary for unforeseen circumstances; meetings running overtime, weather delays, cancelled flights (which in this part of the world was not uncommon), etc. Any or all of these would cause delays and possible changes in the trip agenda.

Trying to be prepared for all of these changes was a challenge for the Hawk, but a lot of fun to overcome, most times. This was one of those times.

On the way from Muscat to Amman, Jordan, our flight was routed through Dubai, UAE and we arrived in the early evening. We planned to check into a hotel near the airport, have dinner, get a good night's sleep and catch an early morning flight on to Amman. Everything was on track until we got off the aircraft and had to clear Customs at the airport.

I was in the lead and gave the agent my passport. He promptly stamped it, and I was on my way through to the other side of a glass partition into the main area of the airport. As I reached the other side and turned around, much to my surprise and dismay, the General was not there. I looked back through the glass and saw Big Red's face getting redder and redder. The next thing I knew, two armed security guards were escorting the General away from the counter.

He started pointing at me and shouting "Get me out of here!" I quickly tried to go back into the Customs area to find out what the problem was. The Customs agent explained to me that the General was in the country illegally. His passport had the one-time entry visa that had already been used during our visit to Abu Dhabi, UAE. Now we were in Dubai trying to spend the night and the General had no visa to leave the airport. He was trapped in a Customs room until the Hawk could figure something out.

The Hawk went to the hotel, checked in and started making phone calls back to the States. The General's secretary was in a panic when I told her what had happened, and she made calls to the protocol office, U.S. Customs, and the UAE Embassy in DC trying to find a solution to the problem. In the meantime, I went to get something to eat and had dinner by myself.

After dinner, I called again to the States, but nobody had come up with a solution. I went down to the lobby of the hotel and walked over to the reception desk. The Hawk told the hotel receptionist his sad tale of woe.

The Hawk told how his General was stuck at the airport and asked if the hotel would still honor the reservation if he showed up late. The receptionist then smiled and said there would be no problem holding the room and "Do you need a visa?" I looked at her incredulously and asked "What did you say?" She then explained that there was some arrangement the hotel had, for a one-time fee of $25 that a special visa could be issued for a passenger to spend the night at the airport hotel in Dubai. I quickly paid the fee, grabbed the visa and got a cab to the airport terminal building. I went to the Customs area and presented the visa to the agents. Ten minutes later, Big Red was led out the door. He gave me a smile and thanked me for getting him out, and we returned to the hotel.

It was about midnight and there was nothing open, so we went to the General's room, where he broke out two bottles of Johnny Walker Red out of the mini-bar. He ordered some ice, and when it arrived, he poured both miniatures into a glass. With Scotch in hand, Big Red then told me about his 4 hours in Customs "jail."

Right after being taken away by the Customs officials to a holding room, a very distinguished, dark-skinned man was brought into the same location. The Customs agents locked the door behind them and left.

The General was in civilian clothes for travel due to security concerns, and the man had no idea whom he was locked up with. He started a conversation with the General and told Big Red he was a Somali doctor, living in Switzerland, trying to return to Somalia. On his way to Mogadishu, he was caught without a legitimate visa for a stopover in Dubai. This was only several months after the *Blackhawk Down* incident and Americans were not big favorites of the Somali people. So here we had an Army General locked in a room with a Somali, who could have been anything other than a doctor.

The Hawk actually met Farah Aideed one day when he was in charge of the airport in Mogadishu. Farah Aideed visited the airport when the first civilian airliner landed providing commercial service between Mogadishu and Nairobi, Kenya. It was the first commercial flight in over two years and was a big deal at the time. Farah Aideed looked like a distinguished professor or an elderly grandfather and not some megalomaniac killer. The Americans discovered much later how deadly this benign-looking man really was. Although the doctor looked quite distinguished, Big Red never told him what he did for a living. It was a little bit startling, though, that of all the people the General could be locked up with, he would get a Somali.

At the time, we still had many American soldiers in Somalia and the General was the Commander of all Special Forces there. Special Forces teams conducted recon missions and Navy SEAL snipers provided security at the airport and seaport in Mogadishu. The Somali doctor had a prime target in Big Red, had he only known who was in the room with him. This all happened because of a passport screw-up, but Big Red and Hawk could only laugh about it later, as they told the story upon their return to the States.

One of the major success stories which gave Big Red particular delight dealt with King Abdullah, the present-day leader of Jordan. When Big Red and I were conducting our visits, I was responsible for setting up meetings with his counterparts in the countries within our area of responsibility. At the time of our visit to Jordan, Abdullah was then-Prince Abdullah and he was a Brigadier General in charge of all Jordanian Special Forces. He was only 33 years old; his mother was English and his father was the late King Hussein, ruler of the Hashemite Kingdom.

Abdullah was educated at Sandhurst, a famed military academy in the United Kingdom, and spoke the King's English perfectly. He was a charming young man and took us out to dinner at a local Italian restaurant on our first night in Amman, the capital of Jordan.

The next day, Big Red and I visited his headquarters

and training facility. We received briefings and observed his men conducting a Special Operations demonstration exercise. The exercise was an assault on a bus with hostages on board. Abdullah's men "killed" all the bad guy hostage-takers, although two of the hostages were also "killed" in the assault. However, the demonstration was considered a great success, and we proceeded to have a celebration meal of goat meat and rice.

After lunch, we adjourned to the Prince's office and asked Abdullah to come for a return visit to Tampa, Florida, an invitation he readily accepted. During his discussions with Big Red, which I was privy to because I was considered the General's escort and was allowed to attend all the briefings, Abdullah requested a myriad of U.S. military equipment for his men. Some of the items he asked for included Blackhawk helicopters, laser-guided scopes, lightweight Kevlar bullet-proof vests and helmets, the latest NVG technology and the list went on and on.

Jordan is a relatively poor country and was always looking for assistance of any kind. Big Red told me that Abdullah had just returned from a visit to North Korea asking for military equipment. The American government was not very happy with him or his father for making such a visit. However, we did have fruitful discussions and kept the doors open for future exercises to be conducted by American Special Forces soldiers on Jordanian soil. It was a valuable area for our soldiers to train in, and became even more important as the looming showdown with Saddam Hussein would become a reality.

A few years later, King Hussein passed away and

Prince Abdullah inherited the throne, becoming King Abdullah II. He remained a staunch ally of the United States over the years and helped facilitate the invasion of Iraq during the second Gulf War by providing airfields and bases in Jordan to support the war effort.

The Hawk kept in touch with Big Red over the years, and once at a party together the General made the following remark, which I thought was kind of funny but thoughtful and maybe truthful at the same time. He said, "We did a good job with Abdullah. We got him promoted!"

Sometimes Big Red got a big kick out of the Hawk's discomfort on their travels. Army people are used to living in the field, or "in the bush", as they called it. The creature comforts of home were not available to guests. Air Force pilots, however, were not usually exposed to these kinds of living conditions. The typical Air Force pilot was usually a pampered Prima Donna, regardless of what aircraft he flew.

The Air Force motto was "to fly and fight and don't you forget it." Therefore, pilots were treated very well and usually stayed in nice quarters or hotels whenever traveling away from home base. The size of the room, the size of the bed, the amount of booze in the mini-bar, all had to meet certain requirements for an Air Force pilot to receive the proper crew rest before he "strapped on his jet" for his next flight. So when Big Red and the Hawk were deployed to Egypt for a desert exercise and put in a tent with cots for sleeping arrangements, the Hawk was a little disgruntled.

The Hawk was really taken aback the next morning, as he and the General got dressed for the day's first briefing. To look presentable, shaving was still required, but the only water available was from a canteen on their web belts. The water had gotten quite cold overnight in the chilly desert environment, and the Hawk was unsure of how to shave. Not being exposed to "harsh" elements like these, he asked the General where the hot water was. A large grin spread across the General's face as he found out what a true "weenie" his new Air Force pilot, Executive Officer was. His comment was, "You're not in Kansas anymore, Toto!" That brought the reality of the situation home to the Hawk. He then proceeded to have the first cold-water shave of his life.

On the visit to Oman, the Hawk provided the General with fodder for another story to regale other officers with at parties. Oman was a phenomenal country in our AOR. Big Red and I landed in Muscat and stayed at a fancy resort hotel situated on the Gulf of Oman. We went for a run on the beach before dinner, and during the run, Big Red provided the Hawk with a history lesson.

In the early '70s, Oman was fighting a Communist insurgency and enlisted the help of the British. The 22 SAS fought side by side with Omani soldiers and provided training and expertise which helped defeat the bad guys. Many of the British soldiers stayed on in Oman and helped develop the Omani Special Forces. When we made our visit, there was, in fact, a British Colonel who was in command of the Omani SF. The General and I were invited to have discussions with him and his staff over lunch.

Upon arrival at his headquarters, we were led into a room where two carpets were laid out. Bowls of rice and plates of strange-looking meat were on them. The General sat down on the one with the Brit Commander and his senior staff guys. The Hawk sat down at the other carpet with the younger and junior staffers. We started to eat.

The young guys with the Hawk hardly spoke English, making it difficult to communicate. The young soldiers spoke Arabic and made gestures with their hands to their mouth, indicating how the Hawk was supposed to eat. The Hawk watched as they grabbed handfuls of rice and meat, squished them into a ball, and popped them into their mouths. A little while later, the servants brought out two additional plates and delivered one to the General's rug and the other to mine. The young guys pointed at the plate and clearly wanted me to eat what was on it. I looked over at the General and he indicated that we were being offered something special. We needed to eat what was being offered so as not to offend our hosts. I reached out and grabbed a piece of the mystery meat, put it in my mouth, and proceeded to chew. It didn't taste too bad, but had a kind of rubbery texture.

All the young soldiers began to smile and then "hoot and holler" in Arabic. I must have had a puzzled look on my face as I was eating, because I watched the Brit CO lean over and whisper something into the General's ear. A broad smile came over Big Red's face, and he told me how proud of me hew was for eating such a delicacy and bringing great honor to us. I thanked him and asked what it was I had eaten. His answer gave me the shock of my

188 / James Danielik

life. I had eaten goat's gonads! It was the goat's balls that actually were so rubbery. Luckily, I had already swallowed them or would surely have gagged and spit them out, creating some sort of international incident!

However, I wasn't the only one to experience something different. On Big Red's special plate were the goat's brains and eyes for him to eat. He managed to eat his delicacies also, and this luncheon provided the basis for another bar story we could tell our colleagues.

I really enjoyed my travels with Big Red. They were not only enlightening, but incredibly fun at times. Not all of the Hawk and Raven adventures were dangerous, but I believe they still made for wonderful stories. It was like a day I spent many years later with another General whom I really admired.

General Mike had a poster hanging in his office at our headquarters in Fort Bragg, which read "Graduate, University of Vietnam." General Mike was very much like the Raven in this respect. The Raven was always telling the Hawk, when asked about his college degree, that he received his degree in soldiering. General Mike indicated the same with his wall-posted degree earned in the jungles of Southeast Asia.

The General had other traits similar to the Raven. His demeanor and temperament were like the Raven in the fact that he was quite stern-looking and could be difficult to get close to, but if you did, you had a friend for life. Another resemblance all three of us shared were the many scars, running like railroad tracks, all over our bodies; General Mike received his from some serious wounds inflicted in

Vietnam as did the Raven. He was also one of those who jumped with the Hawk the day I struck the power lines.

This special day with General Mike, who cut his teeth on airborne units, will always be etched in the Hawk's mind. At six o'clock on a clear and warm August morning, we met on a ramp at Pope AFB and boarded the General's jet. General Mike, his aide and the Hawk flew to a military base near the coast of Virginia.

Upon arrival, we were met by the Commander of a Navy SEAL unit. At a ceremony a few hours later, the General was going to give medals to this Commander's men for daring actions in Bosnia. In the meantime, the SEAL Commander pointed to two Caravans parked nearby that had HALO parachutes and swim fins laid out on the ground next to the planes. We donned our chutes and taped the fins to our legs. A jump brief was conducted and we were then cross-loaded into the two planes. The General and his aide were in the first and I was put in the second. We took off and climbed to 12,000 feet out over the Atlantic Ocean. My SEAL jumpmaster said that as soon as I saw the General exit his plane, I should jump from ours. I did exactly as he said and, when I was under canopy I looked down and saw two cigarette boats making donut circles in the water with their propellers. We maneuvered ourselves near the boats and landed in the water. After unlatching the straps of our chutes, we swam over and climbed aboard the boats. The General and his aide were in one and I was in the other. We were approximately 11 miles from the coast, and our SEAL boat drivers fired up the boats' twin 600-horsepower engines and off we went like rockets, slicing thru the water at over 60 knots. There was no wind and the ocean was calm as could be.

About one mile from the shoreline, the boats came to a stop. We put on our fins and jumped overboard. We commenced swimming to shore where the SEALs compound was located. As we swam, a group of playful dolphins came alongside of us and escorted us to where the waves were breaking. It was a most incredible sight!

After we walked out of the surf, we headed for a shower facility and locker room to cleanup and change into fresh uniforms. We then proceeded to the boat barn where the SEALs kept all of their boats when not in use.

A huge American flag hung from a wall and a set of bleachers was setup for family members. The SEAL team stood at attention and in formation by the time we arrived. The General delivered a very patriotic speech, highlighting their brave acts. He then pinned medals to the chests of those men he just talked about. After the ceremony, we were loaded in a van and driven back to the airport, boarded the General's jet, took off and landed back home around twelve o'clock. What a day I thought to myself! How many Air Force C-141 pilots or any pilots for that matter, were jumping out of planes, riding go-fast boats and swimming with the dolphins all before noon on a normal day of work? I couldn't think of any!

However, life isn't all fun. There are the dark times also.

13 LOSS OF THE RAGMAN AND TEXAS

Sometimes the business the Raven and Hawk were in really sucked. The loss of good friends, colleagues and peers was inevitable due to the dangerous environment we worked in.

Prior to their mission in the Southern California desert that I wrote about previously, the Raven's unit was tasked for a desert mobility exercise in Nevada. Two combat controllers were attached to a reconnaissance element that would go in early by conducting a HALO jump and be a reception party for six C-130s. The CCT guys would setup the infrared beacons to mark the landing strip and communicate with the aircraft with their radios. The aircraft were to land and offload a squadron of Raven's men with an attached squadron from 22 SAS, along with their respective desert mobility vehicles.

The training objective was to drive their vehicles across the desert at night while wearing NVGs. One of the combat controllers was known as the Ragman.

The Hawk remembered one of his first days in the compound and seeing all these tough-looking guys with long hair and bushy mustaches doing physical training every morning in the parking lot outside our building. I asked around the compound as to their identity and told that they were Combat Controllers and Para-rescue men, the Air Force equivalent of Navy SEALs and Army Special Forces. The CCTs and PJs, as they were known, possessed all the physical skills and field training of their sister special ops troops including parachuting, weapons marksmanship, and satellite communications.

These rough-looking dudes began their first day of the week by unrolling rubber mats, laying them on the asphalt, and doing forty-five minutes of non-stop calisthenics, followed by a three-mile run. By Friday, the guys were ready to vent some pent-up energy in a friendly game of two-hand touch football.

I loved to play football; however, there was a stipulation for me. I had to join their morning PT class in order to play on Friday. I freaking hated PT, and their version nearly killed me. I hadn't worked out or kept myself in shape over the years and smoked a pack of cigarettes a day, but I had something over these big brutes. I had some speed, a pair of hands and could catch the long ball.

Catching a couple of "bombs" for touchdowns in the first game I played in allowed the rest of the group to overlook the fact that I only weighed 158 pounds soaking wet. Thereafter, I was never the last guy to be chosen for a team. I guess being a pilot and having some hand-eye coordination helped.

The biggest guys were normally stacked on the line blocking for the quarterback to give him time to throw the ball. The Ragman was one of those on the opposing line in my first game. I thought to myself, "Where did they get this guy?" I thought maybe we were recruiting in downtown Beirut or the West Bank. Actually, he was from Tacoma, Washington.

During the early to mid '80s, personnel in all our units were allowed relaxed grooming standards in order to be able to better blend in with society at large during the heyday of the terrorist. Most terrorists from Europe were longhaired radicals from Germany and Italy, or the more fierce-looking, bearded kind from the Middle East. The bearded ones came from some squalid refugee camp in the Bekaa valley of Lebanon or from the West Bank or Gaza Strip in unrecognized Palestine. These kinds of individuals were easy to recruit and train. All they knew were hatred and killing from the time they were born, and they either held a grudge, had some kind of revenge motive, or just liked the idea of killing innocent people for some misguided cause or principle.

We were sort of terrorists ourselves. We were called counter-terrorists and had to know how to think and act like terrorists in order to understand their motives and modus operandi. We even had to look like them, and the Ragman certainly fit the bill. He was a very large black man with an enormous beard. I could have sworn he was a terrorist whom we had somehow persuaded to see the decadent Western lifestyle as not such a bad way of life.

Raven was the unit Executive Officer at the time of the desert mobility exercise, and he and some of his men were pre-positioned into Texas Lake, high in the Nevada desert.

Texas Lake is a dry lakebed capable of supporting the landing of C-130 cargo aircraft. Raven was providing the administrative support in case the recon team's aircraft had mechanical problems or weather precluded the jump. Raven would be able to put out landing lights and have the radios to provide landing instructions for the C-130 pilots.

The recon team planned a long-range tactical in-filtration, and a CASA aircraft flew them from North Carolina to Nevada for the airdrop. The CASA aircraft orbited for twenty minutes, allowing the sun to set completely, which enabled the team to make a night jump for tactical training. As the team leaped out of the aircraft and began to maneuver into formation, one of the team members had a malfunction and was last seen performing a cutaway. In a cutaway you pull a ripcord that ejects the main parachute and pull another handle to inflate the reserve 'chute.

There was no moon that night, so it was pitch black out. When the recon team rallied at the rendezvous point, the Ragman was nowhere to be found.

The recon team called the Raven on their radios and told him to work the landing zone for the C-130s about to land. The team wanted to look for the Ragman. They searched for him all night. They finally found him the next morning.

It had been so dark that night that the team had been walking all around him, but the visibility had been so poor that they hadn't seen him.

Unfortunately, the Ragman had slammed into the side of a mountain, and his altimeter board had crushed his chest. He also had a broken thigh, and they found him about fifteen feet from the original impact site. There were scratchings in the dirt where the Ragman had dug his good leg into the ground and pushed himself over trying to move. He was found lying on his back, with lifeless eyes looking up. He must have died shortly after, too weak to move or call for help. When the Raven saw him, his most vivid recollection was a dried teardrop running down this fierce black man's face. The salty teardrop had become a small white rivulet.

It was days like these that reminded us we were part of the business, and the business was sometimes painful in a very personal way. The Raven and I lost some good friends and good people over the years in training accidents, although the Raven had experienced many other personal losses earlier during the Vietnam War.

I experienced some losses of fellow pilots over the years also, but not up close and personal like the Raven had in combat.

There is a term fighter pilots use: "Be a dot." It means to be the smallest target possible when engaging enemy fighters. It also seems to explain how a pilot is lost in an aircraft accident. The aircraft usually hits a mountain or crashes into the ground, disintegrating on impact, leaving a smoking hole and pieces no bigger than dots.

My own personal experience was the loss of Texas. Texas was one of the eleven guys in the unit when I first got to Fort Bragg. Texas was a Jolly Green Giant helicopter pilot by trade and also a special ops planner just like the Hawk.

He sat next to me for two years as a co-worker. He became like a brother to me. The day he retired was a beautiful day in the Carolinas without a cloud in the sky.

A retirement ceremony was held in the headquarters building, and was attended by the Commanding General. At the end of the ceremony, everybody came up and congratulated Texas for his honorable twenty years of service. I gave my friend a hug, and he said he would see me down at the trailer. The unit used this trailer, located down on the flight line, to house maintenance teams who worked on our aircraft when they broke. Texas was having a little post-ceremony celebration there.

Texas had a grill set up to cook some hot dogs and hamburgers and there was beer and soda on ice. His wife and two daughters had left a week earlier for their retirement home in Texas. Only his eleven-year old son remained with him, and would ride in the car with his Dad for the trip home.

I was a little delayed getting down to the party by last-minute requirements to sort out at the office. When I finally showed up, I asked where the guest of honor was, and was told he was on a fini flight. "Fini flight" was our term for the last or finished flight.

Unknown to me, there were two Air Force Special Operations Blackhawk helicopters that had been in town training with the Raven's unit. One of the guys in my unit thought it would be a great idea if one of the aircrews could give Texas one last flight in an Air Force special operations helicopter before he became a civilian. With no time to argue, the crew quickly put a helmet on Texas, strapped him into the helo and off they went.

I had gotten there too late to even see him take off. The first hour passed and people ate and drank, not paying too much attention to the time. As more time passed the whispers could be heard starting. Texas's son was at the party, and the first thoughts of trouble were starting to brew in people's minds.

About ten miles off in the distance, a small plume of smoke was seen drifting upwards lazily from the forest of pine trees that surrounded the Fort Bragg military complex. The Deputy Commanding General had also come down to the trailer to say goodbye. He recommended that the son be taken to one of the guys' homes for the time being. Then he made some calls and a search party was launched toward the smoke we were seeing on the horizon.

The tragic news soon filtered back that the smoke was the scene of terrible aircraft wreckage. The unthinkable had happened. The Blackhawk had crashed and was totally destroyed with all passengers killed, including my friend, Texas. The festivities quickly ended and everybody left in a dazed state of condition.

I returned to the office and received one of the toughest orders the Hawk have ever had to accomplish. I was designated to be the escort officer for Texas's son and bring him home to his family.

An Air Force Lear jet, used for dignitaries and Generals on support flights, would fly-in the next morning and pick up the boy and me. We would fly to a military base in Texas and the Deputy Commander of my unit, who happened to be there on vacation at the time, would meet us at the airport.

As the day turned into night, the unit sat around the office and we swapped war stories about Texas with each other. I made a comment that in two years of working side by side, I could not think of a bad thing to say about Texas. I could only remember good things about him. Cobra, who had been asked to deliver the eulogy, used that comment at his funeral service and I wept like a baby. I loved Texas and felt like I had actually lost a member of my own family. He was family, my brother in every sense except blood.

The next morning I dressed in my Air Force blues and picked up the boy at Dave's apartment where he had been taken from the cookout. The night before, Dave had the unfortunate job of telling the kid his father was gone. The boy's eyes were red-rimmed from crying all night.

We flew mostly in silence to Texas and were met by my Deputy Commander upon landing. The three of us then drove out to Texas's farm, where Texas planned to spend his retirement years. As we walked through the door, Texas's wife and two daughters met us. Their hysterical crying that followed was so emotional and draining that I was completely overwhelmed by it.

I spent the rest of the day and part of the evening trying to provide some comfort and support to the family, as well as I could.

That night I drove back to the base and spent a restless night at the Bachelor Officers' Quarters (BOQ).

In the morning, I drove out to base operations near the flight line and picked up the unit Operations Officer (who was Texas's and my immediate supervisor). Silver, as we called him, brought with him an American flag to deliver to the family. The crash-site wreckage had left absolutely no remains to return home, so an American flag representing Texas was brought to the farm. A funeral ceremony was quickly planned and all of Texas's family and friends from this rural community came to the church in an outpouring of support. The church was totally filled, and the overflow crowd stood outside in the blazing Texas heat as a sign of respect.

In an ironic twist, the Air Force helicopter guy whom Texas had replaced in our unit was stationed at the nearby base, working personnel issues. With his clout, Rotor coordinated a formation fly-by of several huge Special Operations Jolly Green Giant helicopters like the ones Texas had flown. The helicopters had been out West training and just happened to be on the return flight to their home base in Florida. As the aircraft over-flew the funeral ceremony at tree-top level, one of the aircraft broke up and out of the formation, signifying the missing man. A fresh round of tears instantly swept over the crowd of people.

Many years later, the Hawk had the good fortune to command this same unit. One of the success stories I was able to accomplish on my watch was the dedication of the unit's new building. The unit had grown in size over the years and needed additional offices and planning areas. A new building had been erected since I had last served in the unit.

On a rather cool and breezy June morning, a ceremony was held to honor my late friend. A handsome granite marker engraved with Texas's name was placed outside the entrance to the building. His widow, parents and all his children were able to attend and unveil the marker in a beautiful and moving emotional event. Hopefully, it brought some closure to the family and provided a legacy for the unit.

An honor guard presented the American flag and the 82nd Airborne chorus sang *God Bless the USA* and *The Wind Beneath My Wings*.

These are the words I used to express my thoughts about the significance of Texas and his contributions to the unit.

"I want to thank the Good Lord for providing this beautiful blue Carolina day. I'm sure Texas is with us here also today. This is a time of celebration for a great American. You knew him as father, son, husband, officer and friend, but I knew him as Texas. He sat by my side, both in garrison and when deployed, for over two years. I probably spent more time than anyone with him for that that period of time and came to love him like family. I would like to share some of that time with you.

"We were second-generation guys who came into the unit together during the infancy of the air component. Texas was more senior than I and he became not only a good friend, but a mentor also. He was one of those guys that could go for two or three days with no sleep, get that haggard, black circles under your eyes and stubby-growth-beard look that those in this community are very familiar with, and was still able to continue to plan effectively.

"He was the unit rotary-wing planner and worked both Air Force and Army helicopters for our missions. He was one of the best, if not the best, planners I have ever seen and had a great working relationship with all units, whether Army or Air Force. He had not an ounce of bias in his bones and I marveled at his ability to work with people. I learned from him how to win the hearts and minds of pilots, which is usually a very difficult thing to do. Pilots all have "type A" personalities and they think they are always right. Texas would talk to them with that easy smile and a big old stogie hanging out of his mouth. The pilots just couldn't help themselves. They warmed to him and followed his guidance and direction. That was the Texas I knew.

Back in the mid-'80s, when American hostages were being held in Beirut, our unit was called to send a helicopter planner to the Mediterranean and ride an aircraft carrier. When the time came, a helicopter with Texas on board launched from the carrier and landed in Beirut and picked up the Reverend Weir and flew him to freedom. Texas was then able to escort the Reverend Weir in another aircraft to Sigonella NAS, Italy, for turnover to competent authorities. Texas was the first American the Reverend Weir had spent time with in many years, and we were so proud to have a guy from the unit be involved in this operation, and, having it be Texas was the right guy. That's the Texas I remember.

"We camped and fished together also. One morning, Texas, Cobra and I went out fishing in Texas's boat on Lake Jordan and caught sixty bream. It wasn't like we were catching 10-pound bass, but it was so much fun. We were like little kids in a candy store, laughing and cutting up. Again, that's the Texas I will always remember.

"At his eulogy 12 years ago, Cobra quoted me as saying I couldn't think of anything but good in the time I knew him, and that's the same way I feel today. The times I had with Texas were always good. That's what makes today so special. I get to celebrate a great American not only publicly but personally as well. I want to thank the family for being here. I want to thank the Pope Honor Guard and the 82nd Airborne chorus. And all others who helped make this ceremony a reality. God bless you and God bless America."

It was these difficult times that really bonded all Special Ops people together. The loss of close friends and colleagues was emotional and tough on those left behind. Working in such close quarters and doing such stimulating work, which only a select few would ever experience, was both rewarding and challenging at the same time. You made such close and lasting friendships, but you could also lose those friendships in the blink of an eye.

The rewards were the friendships, and the challenge was to carry on, in spite of the grief and anger generated by the loss of good friends in tragic accidents. The Raven and the Hawk experienced both.

14 THE HUNT FOR UBL

Out of the carnage that was Desert One, the failed rescue attempt of Americans held hostage in the American Embassy in Tehran, Iran, America's "terrorists" were born. Men with courage, vision and fortitude created units, provided equipment and commenced training America's version of terrorists. They had to look, speak, act, think and be just like the guys we were after. The men who volunteered, who were then selected and trained, became an awesome capability and national asset.

The problem was "when, why, where and how" to employ this enormous and powerful weapon. The United States considered itself the kinder, gentler nation. All men are created equal, certain inalienable rights, freedom of speech, etc., etc., were some of the foundations upon which this great nation was built. These are the principles that Americans are taught from the beginning of their schooling. Woven from this fabric are the Americans who became doctors, lawyers, baseball players, teachers as well as the people the Raven and I worked with –America's trained terrorists.

When we trained and exercised against potential and perceived threats, we created as much realism as we possibly could. Role-players simulating hostages and bad guys, chemical labs, trains, planes and cruise liners, were hired, rented, leased or built; various scenarios were drawn up. A small cell of personnel called the Exercise Group wielded some mighty power.

Given a huge budget, this group was given the latitude to think of the worst situations that could put Americans in harm's way. They had to sit around and be the bad guys, planning dastardly plots against the kind and benevolent USA and its citizens. Their ultimate mission was to test the skills of America's own counter-terrorist force.

Over the years, scenarios were elaborately brainstormed and locations scouted. Then, on a moment's notice, difficult circumstances were unleashed in order to spark a response from this deadly force. The objective was to kill or capture all the bad guys while saving all the good guys with no loss of life. This training started after Desert One and continues to this day; however, a huge adjustment had to be made.

September 11th, 2001 will be forever etched in everyone's mind due to the incessant replays on television of airliners crashing into the World Trade Center's two magnificent landmark towers.

Having devoted 17 years of my life to this business gives me some measure of credibility. Never in those 17 years could I ever conceive of such a plan. I knew many of the guys who worked in the Exercise Group in my career, who were good, solid Americans trying to be evil. They were incapable or unwilling to think any thoughts close to those that led to the loss of nearly 3,000 lives that day.

As time marched on, the Raven and the Hawk went their separate ways and continued their respective lives' journeys. During these follow-on years, they maintained contact and kept up with each other's private lives and families.

The Raven remained in the military, progressing through the ranks, and was intimately involved in all the United States' battles and wars as the 20th Century turned into the 21st.

The Hawk made a clean break and was fortunate to turn his piloting skills into a job in the outside world flying freighters. The Hawk had actually come full circle. Thirty years before, he started his military career doing the exact same thing. He had been a cargo pilot, but now the outside of his jet was painted in the bright colors of his commercial carrier rather than the Air Force camouflage or flat gray color. The really ironic part was the timing.

The Hawk ended his thirty-year career in October 2000, and less than a year later, the tragic events of 9/11 occurred. The Hawk was domiciled overseas in a third-world country (imagine that) and flying all over Southeast Asia. He was exactly half-way around the world from the death, destruction and horror being experienced in his own hometown. Less than 24 hours after repeatedly viewing those two planes slamming into the twin towers of the World Trade Center, he flew on a company flight.

The world continued to turn on its axis, the digits continued to flash on his wristwatch, and it was business as usual for the company. The freight had to move, and pilots had to fly the planes that carried the cargo.

It became a totally surreal experience for the Hawk. In less than one year, he made the transition from being the hunter, the marksman, and the counterterrorist to become the target. Those 19 fanatics who took over the four planes on 9/11 killed the FAs (First or Lead Attendant) by slashing their throats with box cutters, which they had smuggled on board. The terrorists then took the keys to the cockpit doors off the lifeless bodies.

They quickly opened the cockpit doors and with those same bloody box cutters, slashed the throats of the two pilots manning the flights. The pilots and First Attendants never had a chance. Never expecting or being exposed to something so violent would not prepare them to defend themselves. It all happened in the blink of an eye.

The terrorists had been planning and practicing this cowardly act for over a year. The total elapsed time was probably less than a minute from the time the terrorists arose from their seats in unison, until they were in control of those four jets.

As my friends and family called and asked me how I felt or what was I thinking, I remember feeling numb. I was some kind of robot going through the motions, operating my jet on pure instinct and some deep-seated, repetitive memory cells.

I actually had a peripheral relationship with two of the eight pilots murdered. A Captain on the American Airlines flight out of Boston (which crashed into one of the towers) and the First Officer on the United Airlines flight (which crashed in the Pennsylvania countryside after a vicious battle between the passengers and terrorists), were both former C-141 pilots.

The Captain had served in the same squadron as the Hawk at an East Coast base. The Captain was older and more senior to the Hawk, but one of the Hawk's classmates from Undergraduate Pilot Training (UPT) 30 years prior was based with this Captain at the same time and actually flew as a copilot for him in the C-141. American Airlines, in another twist of irony, hired the Hawk's classmate when he retired from the Air Force. The Hawk's father had also been an employee of American Airlines.

The Hawk's good friend, the Scorpion, who followed into the Hawk's jobs in Special Operations, later became a C-141 squadron commander. A young Captain in his squadron had reached the top of the pyramid and become a SOLL II pilot, like the Hawk and the Scorpion had been earlier in their careers.

This young man was destined for a bright future in the Air Force had he elected to stay. The Scorpion tried to convince the young hotshot pilot to stay in the service when his commitment was up, but he was unable. The young man ended his Air Force career and was hired by United Airlines, to eventually become the co-pilot on the United Airlines jet on that fateful day.

Soon after 9/11, Richard Reid, the "Shoe Bomber" who attempted to blow up an American Airlines flight from London to Boston, was overcome and defeated by the flight crew. The Captain of this flight was a contemporary of the Hawk and served at the same time at their Southern California base thirty years ago. Hans received a special award from the Daedalians because of his actions. Talk about a small world.

The United States government is now considering preemptive actions against terrorists and rogue states. In the past, the idealistic U.S. would have attempted to negotiate with a sovereign nation, but no longer. We will not have another 9/11. The times have really changed. Security procedures, levels, and checks impact on personal liberties, a dramatically altered scene in the U.S.

The thinking has become so drastic that one of the Captains, who the Hawk flies with at his commercial carrier, came up with a new and quite novel proposal. In flight one day, the Hawk had casually mentioned that the guys he worked with in his military career were unable to imagine any scenarios that would be so incredibly evil. This Captain, whom Hawk nicknamed "BA" (Bad Ass), later sat across from him at breakfast one morning and nonchalantly asked him if he would like to join his vigilante group.

The Hawk was drinking coffee and reading the morning newspaper, detailing the deaths of 12 Nepalese in Iraq by beheading and mass execution. These 12 men only came to Iraq to be cleaners and cooks, and they lost their lives because of it.

In another article, some other Iraqi militant fringe group was holding seven truck drivers hostage. They all called themselves The Army of something; The Army of the Revolution for the Liberation of Iraq, the Army of the Martyr Brigades, The Army of the New Iraq, The Army of Jihad, or some such nonsense.

So as Hawk was reading and BA asked him about joining his vigilante group, the Hawk's morbid curiosity got the better of him, and he asked, "What vigilante group?" BA then proceeded in vivid detail to explain his version of the new, Western-mandated justice.

Looking the Hawk straight in the eye, BA said, "My vigilante group, named the Body Liberation Army (BLA), (which will become self-evident here shortly), would travel around the world and snatch Muslim Clerics. The group would be dressed in masks and tight-fitting, surfer rash guards, colored red, white and blue. They would have a surfer's long board standing straight up in a pile of sand taken from the dunes of the Saudi Arabian desert".

"One of the vigilante members would crank up a chain saw (Black and Decker, no doubt!) and, in full view of a video recorder, cut the cleric's head off! After the body was liberated and the Cleric's body was flopping on the ground like a fish out of water, the bloody stump of a head would be placed on a Koran and placed on top of the long board. The entire video would be sent to Al Jazeera, the Arab television station, to be broadcast for all to see."

The Hawk sat there absolutely dumbfounded, his jaw

dropping to the ground in incredulity as BA told him all of this. The Hawk asked, "Is this what we have become? An eye for an eye, a tooth for a tooth?" BA replied, "No! A head for a head!"

The Hawk couldn't begin to fathom such thoughts, but this guy could. To him, it actually reflected the New World Order. Anything goes he said, "We need to be as bad as they were. We need to think as evil as they do in order to defeat them."

My goodness, the Hawk was in total shock. For a moment, he joked around with BA and went along with his way of thinking. The Hawk remembered back in the 1980's when Americans were being taken hostage in Beirut and killed or held captive for years. A little-known incident that occurred about the same time involved the same terrorist group taking some Russians hostage. The Russians actually sent their Special Operations troops to Beirut, captured family members of the hostage takers and proceeded to cut off their genitals and send the parts back to their families. The message was relayed that the Russians would continue to cut off more parts until their hostages were released. The Russians got their hostages back, pronto! The American way of thinking at the time couldn't or wouldn't conceive of such a notion.

But now, 20 years later, after nearly three thousand were killed on 9/11 and with more Americans being killed in Afghanistan and Iraq, the kid-gloves are off. Americans are serious, and just how serious is reflected by BA and his recruitment into the BLA.

Muslim extremists are no more representative of the

Islamic world than Timothy McVeigh, the Oklahoma City bomber, the Columbine child-shooters or the Ku Klux Klan are representative of ordinary Americans. If we surrender our values and our liberties, those ideals that mark us as Americans, in order to defeat them, then we lose what we are. We stop being American and the terrorists have won. It's a hard call because only terrorists have the easy answers. Those for whom freedom and democracy ring out loud and are worth defending and dying for will never have easy answers to give.

The Hawk actually had a more favorable response from the Scorpion that brought him some peace and closure. The Scorpion had also remained in the military like the Raven, but had gone back to the regular Air Force. Scorpion's last job in Special Ops had been as Deputy Commander to the Hawk, in the unit that they had both previously served in as young action officers. When he left that job, the Scorpion put on his Air Force blues and went to work, no longer involved in Special Ops at all.

The Scorpion left the unit only a short time before the Hawk retired. The Hawk and the Scorpion had a very close personal relationship as well and kept in contact over the years.

The Hawk, feeling desperate after 9/11, called the Scorpion to see how he was holding up. This was around November 2001 and our old unit had been involved in the initial assault against the Taliban in Afghanistan. The Scorpion replied, "I'm fine." The Hawk asked how he felt "not being in the middle of all the action." The Scorpion explained it to the Hawk this way:

"Hey", he said, "We had our turn in the barrel. We were able to accomplish great and wonderful deeds on our watch. It's the next generation's turn."

We were the ones, as Commander and Deputy Commander, who hired young hotshots into the unit, trained them and let them go. It was their turn now.

He continued, "We can be proud of their accomplishments and live vicariously through them as they plan and execute special missions throughout Afghanistan," (and later Iraq).

We would be there in spirit, if not in the flesh, and we had to take pride in the fact that we left the unit in good stead. These young action officers were just like us when we came into the unit 20 years earlier. They were full of "piss and vinegar" and able to stay up for days at a time, and live off the adrenaline rush of being involved in special operations. They were the new combat junkies, the new Hawks, the new Ravens.

The saddest part of this entire episode is the realization that 9/11 might have been prevented. After the twin embassy bombings in Kenya and Tanzania in 1998, the Hawk was seriously engaged in an effort to eliminate Usama Bin Laden. Through intelligence sources, Bin Laden's residence was pinpointed in Afghanistan. The Taliban harbored this fugitive bastard and provided him safe sanctuary.

A special operations plan, which was well-conceived and involved only a few special operations units, was rehearsed over and over again. The plan would require the destruction of Bin Laden's residence, when we had hard and fast intelligence that he was there. Unfortunately, there was a potential for "collateral damage." The weapons we planned to use to destroy Bin Laden's residence were very accurate, but not accurate enough for the politicians in Washington.

After showing videotapes of a replica of Bin Laden's residence being totally destroyed, including the destruction of some neighboring residences, the green light was never given. It did not matter that Bin Laden had been involved in numerous terrorist acts against Americans in Somalia, the Khobar Towers, the U.S.S. Cole bombing, the two embassies, and elsewhere, the powerful men of Washington would not employ this deadly force. The potential loss of innocent lives in order to eliminate one individual was unacceptable. The Nervous Nellies in D.C. were afraid that if innocent women and children, even if they were Bin Laden's relatives, were killed and the press found out, watch out! The media folks would have a field day and make us out to be "baby killers!" It would be Vietnam all over again.

Therefore, the plan was shelved, and we never got the SOB! He continued to live in the comfort and safety of his Taliban haven. Life went on, the operation was forgotten and the politicians got on with being politicians. More important issues, like a presidential election and getting re-elected became the priority and UBL was off the radar scope. As much as Richard Clark would try to convince the Commanders-in-Chief to eliminate this threat, UBL was allowed to live, and we all know the results. The hunt for UBL continues to this day and was a major campaign issue in the 2004 presidential election. I am sure the Raven's and Hawk's old units continue to search and plan and still hope to this day to terminate his activities.

15 A SACRED TRUST

As the vehicle made a left turn, the SEAL sniper focused his scope. He could actually see the terror in the driver's eyes, and the beads of sweat glistening on his forehead as his acuity, through the long-range scope began to adjust to the environment. The sniper moved the weapon ever so slightly to the right, and the handgun pointed at the back of the driver's head became visible.

The sniper continued his slow scan and the hand, arm and head of the terrorist came into sight in the crosshairs. As the vehicle slowed due to the traffic and a stop light ahead, the sniper began to take measured breaths. He only had a very small window of opportunity. He must not fail. All that training, all those hours spent on the range - now it was the moment of truth.

People he didn't know were counting on this lone warrior. The hostage's wife, children, parents, brothers, sisters and co-workers were all, unknowingly, praying for the success of this single act of violence.

The vehicle stopped.

The sniper's finger rested lightly on the trigger. In his ear a small transmitting microphone uttered the words, "Execute! Execute! Execute!"

The sniper's forefinger provided the four pounds of pressure necessary to commence the following sequence of events: The trigger activated the firing mechanism, which struck the back end of the shell casing; instantaneously, a 5.56-millimeter piece of steel, traveling at one mile per second, entered the left side of the terrorist's head below the temple and above the ear, leaving a perfectly round hole the size of a marble.

The exit wound was much more devastating. A large piece of the man's skull, along with his brain tissue, hair, scalp, and right ear, was ripped from his head and impacted on the passenger-side window pane. A misty, fine spray of red blood covered the back seat, and the driver felt it on the back of his neck.

At that moment, the sniper took a breath, closed his eyes, and thanked his God for giving him the courage, fortitude and strength to carry out such an act.

One day on the range, as the Hawk's career was coming to a close, he had the honor to narrate another special operations capability demonstration. This demo was conducted for the United States Attorney General, the Head of the FBI, the Secretary of Defense, four Senators from the Senate Armed Services Committee and all their staff and security detail. They were all flown in by helicopter to this well-protected, secret and secure location in North Carolina. They would see first hand how accurate and well-trained our forces were.

It was on just such a day and in the same circumstances, fifteen eventful years before, that the Raven and I had first laid eyes on each other. This was where our journey had begun as we took the torch from those who went before us and here we were about to pass it on to the young men who expertly checked their armaments around us, a torch lit by a sacred trust each man had in the others.

For two straight days prior to the final demonstration, the Hawk practiced his delivery and the timing of the events to be displayed. He stood at a lectern with a microphone and a pre-drafted, detailed explanation of the capabilities our nation's highest leaders were about to witness. We wanted to ensure the exact sequence of events would occur as the script was read. We also wanted to make certain all precautions, safety concerns and margins for error were taken into account.

On the day before the actual demonstration, our Commanding General and his entourage followed the same itinerary as the government officials. The General was to view more than a practical demonstration of the awesome skills these men brought to their mission. He would stop, ask questions, receive answers and move on, satisfied in our abilities to plan and execute these capabilities so vital to the safety of our nation. The point of this story is to address the sacred amount of trust we place on these extraordinary and relatively young men performing extraordinary skills.

As the General watched from a small berm overlooking an open field, a young Navy man drove a pickup truck slowly by. In the back seat, visible through the king cab window opening, was a human silhouette. The driver then proceeded to head down a dirt road paralleling the open field.

Off to the left of us, where we were standing on the berm, stood a three-story tall wooden structure that looked like an apartment building. Situated in a window on the third floor were a SEAL sniper and his weapon of choice: an M4 with a long-range scope.

As the Hawk read the script describing the hostage-taking scenario unfolding before us, the driver continued his slow drive down the dirt road. At approximately two hundred meters (more than two football fields placed end to end), the truck made a left turn and drove perpendicular to our position on the berm. The driver slowly came to a stop. A single gunshot rang out from the wooden building and echoed across the range. It was at the precise moment that the Hawk was reading about the SEAL sniper receiving the "Execute" order from his superior that the shot was fired.

The pickup truck then started to move again. After traveling a short way, the truck made a left turn on another dirt road that paralleled the first one on the other side of the field and headed toward us. The timing continued to be crucial as Hawk completed the briefing. It would increase the drama and impact of the moment.

The driver then made another left turn in front of the berm and drove by us, quickly making a complete U-turn to drive by once again with the silhouette visible in the window. However, there was one major notable difference. Perfectly centered in the head of the cardboard silhouette was a hole, the size of a dime. The sniper on the third floor took the shot that demonstrated a deadly capability to our country's highest leaders. Leaving the demonstration, our nation's influential men had yet another powerful impression indelibly marked by precisely timed visuals and aural sounds.

The General watched the complete sequence of events unfold before him and had only one question for the young Navy SEAL Lieutenant, who was the overall commander of the men conducting the activities on this range.

He asked, "What protection does the man driving the pickup have?"

The rock-solid, blue-eyed, blond-haired action figure answered quickly and succinctly, but perfectly serious, "Sir, he will have ear protection."

The General, the Hawk and all others looked at each other in amazement. We thought that maybe the driver's door window was bulletproof, or maybe he was wearing a bullet proof vest, or something along those lines. The SEALs gave the guy driving the truck two spongy ear plugs to prevent the sound of the bullet whipping by three feet from his head from causing some potential hearing loss!

We were absolutely astounded by the moment, but that demonstrates the kind of sacred trust the men had in each other.

They were so cock-sure of their abilities that their margins for safety were way different than the conservative General's or senior staff officers. The General was thinking about the worst case scenario; the bullet misses the target and something unfortunate and horrible occurs. The SEALs were thinking the shot wouldn't miss and nothing bad could happen.

The trust the Navy driver had in believing the shot would never hit him, and the trust the Lieutenant had in his sniper to actually fire the weapon and not miss. What a moment!

It was times like these that wisdom and experience ruled the day. It also showed the love and respect the men had for the old man, and vice versa.

Eventually, all the necessary safety changes to prevent anything dreadful from occurring were incorporated. The event would still go on as planned, and the young men who conceived this scenario were still able to take the shot. The General just wanted to ensure it was done as safely as possible, but he still believed in their abilities and skills. Therefore, a bullet-proof window was added, and the driver wore a Kevlar helmet and bullet-proof vest.

This demonstration was very much like the one where Hawk had met the Raven for the first time. The Hawk had come full circle and was again at a demonstration, that drove home to him in a flash, the whole thrust of this book. The sacred trust he saw being displayed is exactly what the Raven and the Hawk had developed through the years; a bond and camaraderie, a union of dark souls. They eventually became force multipliers and national assets through a shared sense of purpose. They both had their demons but eventually became the dragon slayers.

They were just two American boys who became men in a dangerous new world and fought their way through a quagmire of asymmetric threats. Both were driven to succeed, and they fed off each other to overcome adversity, obstacles, and evil intentions anywhere in the world.

From their first meeting, they were both touched by a love of the mission and a sense of duty that only they and a few others understand. They found their sacred trust in a closed society, a select, hidden world of special men, a breed like no other.

They were able to share a certain ferocity as young action officers and bring that ferociousness to the new generation of young Turks that continue to fight terrorism today.

Another tremendous benefit to the American military, and ultimately the American public, is all the servicemen who were exposed to this world of a sacred trust. After serving their country in these special assignments, many returned to their respective services, which are conventional and plodding in nature. The exposure to our world would make them better soldiers, sailors, airmen and marines. They would take that sacred trust with them and make their own service better. What a great and wonderful concept.

So, what started as perhaps a chance meeting, evolved into a special and lasting friendship based on a sacred trust. They were able to make a difference on their "watch." The Raven and the Hawk have flown to the mountain top and from their lofty perches were able to view the world from a completely different perspective. Unknown to most people, they remained in the background, quietly making history.

The two Birds of Prey have gracefully moved on, but have left a lasting legacy of which they can both be proud. America can also be proud of their accomplishments.

The Raven and the Hawk have now gone their separate ways, waiting for fate to bring them together again for their next adventure. The uncharted territory they may face some day is still out there.

ACKNOWLEDGMENTS

The support and encouragement I received from many acquaintances helped make this book a reality.

I want to personally thank the following: Susan Danielik, Cole Kuryakin, Bob Coutie, Erin Fielding, Nancy Lemmon, Alex Bangert III, Harry Monroe, and James Valentine.

The inspiration for this book came from Eldon Bargewell. The motivation came from Chuck Pfarrer.

All of my family has always been there for me. Thank you Mom, Dad, Loretta, Lauren, Ryan, Kristin, Shaun, Valerie, Geoffrey, Kathryn Mary, Susan, Alexandra, Trey, and Mady.